CHURCH HISTORY 1
THE FIRST ADVANCE
AD 29–500

TEF Study Guides

This series is sponsored and subsidized by the Theological Education Fund in response to requests from Africa, Asia, the Caribbean, and the Pacific. The books are prepared by and in consultation with theological teachers in those areas. Special attention is given to problems of interpretation and application arising there as well as in the west, and to the particular needs of students using English as a second language.

General Editor: Daphne Terry

ALREADY PUBLISHED

1. A Guide to the Parables

2. A Guide to St Mark's Gospel

3. A Guide to the Book of Genesis

4. A Guide to the Book of Amos

IN PREPARATION

Old Testament Introduction
VOL. 1 History of Israel
 2 The Books of the Old Testament
 3 Theology of the Old Testament

A Guide to Exodus

A Guide to Psalms

A Guide to Isaiah

A Guide to Romans

A Guide to 1 Corinthians

A Guide to Philippians

Church History
VOL. 2 Setback and Recovery
 3 Worldwide

A Guide to Religions

TEF Study Guide 5

CHURCH HISTORY 1
THE FIRST ADVANCE
AD 29-500

JOHN FOSTER

PUBLISHED IN
ASSOCIATION WITH THE
UNITED SOCIETY FOR
CHRISTIAN LITERATURE
FOR THE
THEOLOGICAL EDUCATION FUND

LONDON
S·P·C·K
1972

First Published in 1972
by the S.P.C.K.
Holy Trinity Church
Marylebone Road, London, NW1 4DU

Made and Printed in Great Britain by
The Camelot Press Ltd, London and Southampton

© *John Foster 1972*

[Summary of projected contents of Volumes 2 and 3, likely to be published in 1973 and 1974 respectively:

2. SETBACK AND RECOVERY AD 500–1500
Western civilization falls before invading German tribes, and the new religion, Islam, arises in Arabia.
Yet the Church of the east completes its expansion eastward to China, and the Church in the west wins the west's new populations.
The period ends with more uncertainty, due to abuses within the western Church, but also with promise of unequalled missionary opportunity through discovery of the New World and of new routes about the old world.

3. WORLDWIDE AD 1500 onwards
The Reformation, its divisions, and the demand for the Bible in living languages.
The concurrent Roman Catholic Revival, carrying the Faith along new routes.
The Enlightenment, and new movements in the eighteenth century, from which came the greatest missionary expansion of all, the great period of Bible translation, and the world-wide Church of today.]

SBN 281 02679 3 (net edition)
SBN 281 02696 3 (non-net edition for Africa, Asia, S. Pacific, and Caribbean)

Contents

Illustrations, maps, and charts

ILLUSTRATIONS, MAPS, AND CHARTS

ACKNOWLEDGEMENTS

Thanks are due to the following for permission to reproduce photo-
graphic material: Alinari, Florence; Apostolic Library, Vatican;
British and Foreign Bible Society, London; British Museum, London;
Camera Press Ltd; Du Mesnil du Buisson; John Foster; Mansell
Collection; Rylands Library, Manchester; United Press International;
University Library, Uppsala.

Editor's Note:
The plan and use of this book

WHAT KIND OF CHURCH HISTORY?

Before deciding what kind of Church History textbook to include in the TEF Study Guide Series, teachers of Church History were consulted, in colleges where the book is likely to be used. Some of them are teaching the subject in new and experimental ways: starting from the present-day Church and tracing its history backwards; plunging students straight into fieldwork; planning their own programmed materials for use in the classroom. Clearly no single book could serve all their various needs.

But in a majority of colleges the teaching is on traditional "chronological" lines, with Latourette or books on a similar pattern as the standard general Church Histories most frequently used at degree and diploma level. This, therefore, is the pattern which John Foster has followed in his three-part history. This present volume, *The First Advance*, is Part 1. It covers the first 500 years of the Church's spread, not only westward, but farther into Asia and into Africa.

Part 2, *Setback and Recovery* (AD 500–1500—the "thousand years of uncertainty"), will be concerned among other emphases with the long struggle between Christendom and Islam. In Part 3, Church History *Worldwide* (1500 onwards), the author will examine great movements which have shaped the Church as it is today, culminating in the modern missionary expansion and the growth of autonomous national Churches all over the world. (For fuller details see p. iv.)

SOURCE MATERIALS

A companion reference volume of extracts from original source documents was considered. But W. G. Young's *Handbook of Source Materials for Students of Church History*, published in 1969 by the CLS, Madras, fulfils the need fairly well for the first of the TEF volumes. For this reason, and in order to help students working on their own or without easy access to reference books, it was decided not to issue a separate TEF Source Book. Instead, extracts from the more important sources quoted are included as an integral part of this History.

However, all students who can are strongly advised to obtain for themselves a copy of Young's *Handbook*. Throughout this History the

EDITOR'S NOTE

quotation-reference numbers in bold type correspond to the numbered extracts in Young, and students may find it helpful to read these more extensive extracts in Young as they go along. (For convenience of U.K. readers, copies are stocked by Lutterworth Press, Luke House, Guildford, Surrey, as well as by CLS, Box 501, Park Town, Madras 3, India.)

Quotation-reference numbers in brackets correspond to the numbered list (pp. 168–170 at the end of this book) which gives details of sources of extracts *not* included in Young. Students with access to a library may want to follow up these sources also, and a list of the standard reference books in which they are likely to be found is included in the bibliography, p. 171.

Many of the extracts quoted have been specially translated or abbreviated by the author for inclusion in this book.

MAPS, CHARTS, AND PICTURES

Almost every place-name mentioned in the book can be found on one or other of the *maps* which appear at appropriate points in the text.

The unified *time chart* (pp. 8–11) shows comparative dates of people and events important in the history of the Church in:

(1) The Roman Empire (sub-divided into Latin-speaking West and Greek-speaking East),

(2) Parthia/Persia and neighbouring areas and

(3) India and further east.

The *pictures* show something of life as it was lived by Christians in the first five centuries. Most of them are from the work of artists who themselves belonged to that period.

STUDY SUGGESTIONS

Suggestions for further study appear at the end of each chapter. They are intended to help readers to study more thoroughly and to understand more clearly what they have read. They also provide topics for group research and discussion. They are of two main sorts:

1. *Review questions* on the content of the chapter. These will help readers to check their progress and ensure that they have fully grasped and remembered the ideas discussed and the facts presented. The answers should be written down, and then checked with the Key (p. 172).

2. *Questions for further study, research, and discussion.* These will help readers to understand why things happened as they did; to discover for themselves the links between the life of the Church in the first five centuries after the death and resurrection of Jesus, and the lives of Christians today; and to consider the ways in which their own actions may affect the development of the Church in the future.

The Study Suggestions have not been separated into categories as in some of the other TEF Guides, because many of the review questions seem to lead directly on to a subject for research or a topic for discussion.

Please note that the Study Suggestions are only *suggestions*. Some readers may not want to use them at all. Some teachers may want to use them selectively, or to substitute alternative questions of their own.

The *Key* (p. 172) will enable readers to check their own work on those questions which can be checked in this way. In most cases the Key does not give the answer to a question; it shows where an answer is to be found.

INDEX

The Index (p. 177) includes all the proper names of people and places mentioned and the main subjects dealt with.

BIBLE VERSION

The English translation of the Bible used and quoted in this book is the Revised Standard Version.

ABBREVIATIONS

The following abbreviations are used in the course of the book:

AD	Anno Domini	Jer.	Jeremiah
BC	Before Christ	Mal.	Malachi
Cf.	Compare	Matt.	Matthew
Col.	Colossians	P., pp.	Page, pages
Cor.	Corinthians	Para(s).	Paragraph(s)
Dan.	Daniel	Pet.	Peter
Deut.	Deuteronomy	Phil.	Philippians
E.g.	For example	Ps.	Psalm
Eph.	Ephesians	Rev.	Revelation
Exod.	Exodus	Rom.	Romans
Gal.	Galatians	RSV	Revised Standard Version
Gen.	Genesis	St	Saint
Heb.	Hebrews	Thess.	Thessalonians
I.e.	That is	Tim.	Timothy
Isa.	Isaiah	V., vv.	Verse, verses

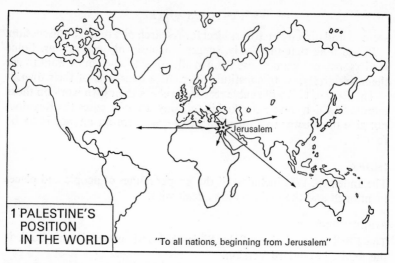

1 PALESTINE'S POSITION IN THE WORLD

Jerusalem

"To all nations, beginning from Jerusalem"

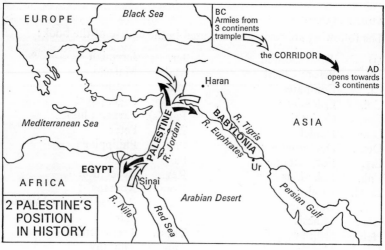

2 PALESTINE'S POSITION IN HISTORY

EUROPE

Black Sea

BC
Armies from
3 continents
trample

the CORRIDOR

AD
opens towards
3 continents

Haran

Mediterranean Sea

PALESTINE

R. Jordan

R. Euphrates

BABYLONIA

R. Tigris

ASIA

EGYPT

Ur

Sinai

Arabian Desert

AFRICA

R. Nile

Red Sea

Persian Gulf

CHAPTER 1

Beginnings

THE PLACE AND THE TIME

The first Christians believed that their religion was good news for all men.

"God so loved the world, that He gave His only Son" (John 3.16). "Repentance and forgiveness of sins shall be preached to all nations, beginning from Jerusalem." (Luke 24.47)

Some of their hearers must have smiled. The wideness of the world seemed so different from the narrow little land where Christianity began.

About the year AD 175, a Greek writer named Celsus wrote a book to show that the Christians' claims were wrong: their religion, he said, was not a great one, but very small. This is what Celsus wrote about Palestine, where Jesus spent all his life:

"If God awoke from a long sleep, and wanted to save all men, do you think he would send to one corner of the world? . . . Only a comic writer would tell us that the Son of God was sent to the Jews." (See W. G. Young *Handbook of Source Materials for Students of Church History*. 1)

To many people, Celsus may have seemed right. Palestine was small. On a map of the world, you hardly notice it (map 1, p. xii). At the time of Christ the whole country measured only 150 miles from north to south, and about 75 miles from east to west. Jesus seldom crossed its frontier. He never went further than He could walk. Few of us spend our lives in so narrow an area.

But Celsus was wrong when he called Palestine a *corner*. Look again at map 1. It was drawn, not for this book, but to show routes of air-lines across the world. We have left out the air-lines, and marked in the position of Palestine. Is Palestine in a corner? We can correct Celsus's words and say, "If God . . . wanted to save all men . . . he would send to just such a *centre*." No country stands more nearly central to the five continents.

So far we have considered geography: i.e. Palestine's position in the world. History too shows that Palestine is central. Look now at Asia and Africa on map 2 (p. xii). The Mediterranean Sea and Red Sea almost separate these two continents; only the small Sinai Peninsula joins them. The narrow corridor between the Mediterranean Sea and the Arabian

1

Desert, which leads to the place of joining, is Palestine. The scene of the history recorded in the Old Testament was Palestine as the corridor between those two continents, Asia and Africa. Or, to be more exact, it was the corridor between two centres of civilization: one Asian, in the Tigris–Euphrates region, i.e. Babylonia; and one African, in the Nile Valley, i.e. Egypt.

Abraham was born at Ur in Babylonia (Gen. 11.31), and later he lived at Haran to the north-west. His "call" (Gen. 12) led him to journey with flocks and herds to find a home in Palestine. But famine drove him south, through the corridor, to the more fertile land of Egypt. A later famine (Gen. 42) brought Abraham's descendants the Israelites, or Hebrews as they came to be called, to Egypt. They lived as foreign tribes in the lands of this Great Power, and became Egypt's slaves.

The great event in Hebrew history is the *Exodus* (Greek for "Way out"), i.e. the escape of the Israelites from Egypt about the year 1200 BC. The tribes crossed the Sinai Peninsula, which is desert, back to the narrow corridor of Palestine through which their ancestors had come. Here they began their troubled attempt to live as a free nation. For a short time, especially under King David, they were independent, but generally they lived in fear of either Babylonia or Egypt. Their country was small and poor. It had a fertile coastal plain, but the remainder was rough hill grazing and the edge of the desert. Palestine's one importance was that it was the only land route between Asia and Africa. This was a dangerous importance, because if Babylonia moved against Egypt, or Egypt moved against Babylonia, Palestine would be trampled in war. The end came in 597 BC when the Asian Great Power, Babylonia, invaded Palestine, burned Jerusalem, destroyed the Temple, and took thousands of the people to exile in Babylonia. The history of the Hebrews might be summed up under the title, "From slavery in Egypt to exile in Babylonia". But this was not the point of view of Old Testament writers. They saw the suffering of their country as God's way of preparing a People for Himself.

"By the waters of Babylon, there we sat down and wept . . .
For there our captors required of us songs . . .
'Sing us one of the songs of Zion!'
How shall we sing the Lord's song in a foreign land?
If I forget you, O Jerusalem, let my right hand wither!" (Ps. 137)

They could not sing glad hymns of praise, but they could, and must, remember their home-land, and believe that God, who made for their ancestors a "way out" from Egypt, could save them from their present troubles. This was the great period of the Messianic Hope, the Israelites' hope for a national *Messiah*, or Saviour.

Palestine was to suffer two further invasions by Great Powers, this time neither African nor Asian, but European. First, in 332 BC, the Greeks came, under Alexander the Great. He moved his armies eastwards, planning to conquer and colonize up to the frontier of India. On the way eastwards he turned south to seize this corridor, Palestine, and go on to the mouth of the river Nile, where he founded the city which still bears his name, Alexandria. His conquests did reach as far as the river Indus.

Then the Romans came. They took over, not only Greece and its remains of Empire, but also much of Greek culture. They continued wide use of the Greek language, and relied on Greek ships and sailors. The Romans extended their Empire along both shores of the Mediterranean, of which the northern shore was largely European, and the southern shore African. In 64 BC they joined their northern and southern provinces by taking Palestine, the corridor between the two. Thus by the time of Christ, Palestine's central position had led to her invasion by Great Powers of three continents, Asia, Africa, and Europe (see again map 2, p. xii).

The Acts of the Apostles begins the history of a new age, when Palestine's central position was used by God in a new way. The Apostles themselves at first did not realize this: "Lord, will you at this time restore the kingdom to Israel?" (Acts 1.6). The Lord's reply changed the subject. He did not speak of the kingdoms of this world, Asia, Africa, Europe, pressing upon this little central land and bringing its destruction. A new kind of Kingdom had begun in this little central land, which was now to be carried to Asia, Africa, Europe. "You shall be my witnesses . . . to the end of the earth" (Acts 1.8).

The *place* was important: "Beginning from Jerusalem" (Luke 24.47). The *time* was important too: "Jesus came . . . preaching the gospel of God, and saying, 'the time is fulfilled'" (Mark 1.14). St Paul used a similar phrase: "The time had fully come" (Gal. 4.4). Both statements mean that God had been preparing, and the preparation was complete.

Christians who lived at the time of Christianity's first swift advance (up to the year AD 250), and who themselves played a leading part in that advance, saw that God had prepared for it in three ways:

1. Roman peace and Roman communications;
2. Greek language and Greek thought;
3. Hebrew religion.

ROMAN PEACE AND ROMAN COMMUNICATIONS

One of these leading Christians was Origen, so we need to know who he was. He was born of Christian parents in Alexandria in 185. He received a good Greek education, first from his father and then at the Christian college founded by Pantaenus, who later went as a missionary

1.1   "Conditions for travel had never been so good." (p. 5)
Floor mosaics now at Palestrina in Italy show what Roman travellers of the first or second century might have seen as they journeyed up the Nile by boat on their way to Ethiopia or India.

to India (p. 42). Origen took the place of his master Clement as head of this college in 202 when he was only seventeen years old. In 231 he moved to Caesarea in Palestine, where he continued similar work. He was one of the greatest saints, and one of the most learned men, famous among non-Christians as well as Christians. After imprisonment and torture, he died in 256 (p. 74). He had met learned men, students, and travellers from many lands, and had himself travelled west to Rome and east to Arabia.

Origen had no doubt that Roman peace and communications had a part in God's purposes.

"God was preparing the nations for his teaching . . . Jesus was born in the reign of the Emperor Augustus (27 BC—AD 14), who brought many kingdoms into one Roman Empire. Wars between rival kingdoms would have hindered the spread of the teaching of Jesus over the whole earth." (Young 2)

The Roman peace was closely connected with communications. The Romans built military roads, with stone foundations, steep hills cut away, and rivers bridged, so as to move soldiers quickly and to keep the peace. Many Roman roads are used to this day in Europe and North Africa. Because of these roads, there was peace; and because of peace, the roads were used by many people besides soldiers.

An official or a rich man would travel in a horse-drawn coach, his servants following with the baggage; or (like the African official in Acts 8) in a lighter carriage, with a servant behind and room on the seat beside him. A man of the middle class would ride, with a servant perhaps, on horses or mules (see p. 4). A poor man, as today in east Mediterranean and north African lands, would ride a donkey; or would just hitch up his garments and walk, hoping for a lift perhaps on a waggon bringing African corn from the ports, wool from Spain, cloth or glass made in Egypt, or hides from north Europe. A traveller on the roads might meet students going abroad for study, conjurers and clowns with a travelling show, a teacher with a book which he had written or with ideas which he wanted to make known, and, of course, soldiers going to change the guard on a distant frontier. Travel was not speedy— sixty to seventy miles a day for those who rode anything faster than a donkey—but it was so easy and safe that some people travelled for pleasure. Conditions had never been so good, would not be so good again for many centuries, and would never be better till the coming of railways and steamships in the nineteenth century.

Sea-travel on the Mediterranean was too crowded to be comfortable. Even the larger ships were less than 200 feet long. On St Paul's ship described in Acts 27.37, there were 276 people. Notice the variant reading in a footnote in the RSV: "76"—probably altered from 276 by later copyists who thought 276 impossible. But there are records of other cases like this. Some passengers must have had "standing room only".

The road system was not so wonderful outside the Mediterranean lands, but there were well-established routes followed by Roman traders and travellers.

A book called *Periplous* (Greek for "The Voyage"), written about AD 60, describes routes and ports and shipping from the east end of the Roman Empire, through the Red Sea to the Arabian Sea, then down the east coast of Africa or across to east Asia.

The first stage of the journey was from Alexandria, 500 miles by boat up the Nile to Koptos (map 5, p. 110); then a week by camel over the desert, with watering places provided, to Myos Hormos (Greek: "Mussel Harbour") on the Red Sea coast. Ships going south from there called at Adulis, which was then the port for Ethiopia just as Massawa, a little to the north, is today; then on to Mocha, in the Yemen, at the tip of Arabia. This port is described as:

> "crowded with Arab dhows and sailors. They carry on trade sending their own ships both down the African coast, and across to India."
> (Young 4)

The African trade reached as far as Zanzibar, and somewhere further south where, the writer says, "the unexplored ocean curves around towards the west". This seems to hint at a possible route round South Africa.

The book adds much more about India, where the chief port was Broach (map 5) in Gujarat; other ports mentioned being Kalyan, near modern Bombay, and Cranganore in Kerala, which had a great trade in pepper.

In about AD 45 a sailor with the Greek name of Hippalus, so the book tells us, had ventured to set his course from Arabia straight across the Arabian Sea, instead of coasting around it. He used the south-west wind, which blows strongly from June to September, to carry him swiftly across. This meant a stormy and dangerous crossing, but shortened the journey by weeks.

Beyond these ports, the book mentions Ceylon, with its pearls and tortoise-shell; ports at the mouth of the Ganges on India's east coast; further east, Malaya; and further still, China, where

> "inland from the coast there is a very great city called Thinae, from which come silk thread and cloth. This country is not easy to reach; few come from there, and seldom." (Young 4)

A journey from the east Mediterranean by the Red Sea to India, or down the east African coast, must have been something of an adventure. But Strabo, a Greek traveller and writer of about AD 7, says that both journeys were made by "great fleets . . . bringing most valuable cargoes back to Egypt". After AD 45 when the daring seamanship of Hippalus shortened the journey time, trade with India again increased. A merchant of Alexandria might go to India, buy his spices, perfumes, precious stones, muslins, and silver, and reach home again having taken only half a year. We have said that land journeys within the Roman Empire were so safe and easy that many people travelled for pleasure. Even in this wider sphere we hear of such travellers, e.g. Meropius of Tyre (see p. 106), who visited India and even took with him two young boys who were his pupils. The journey was part of their education, and he saw that they did not neglect their ordinary studies on the way.

The last item in the *Periplous* was a brief account of China. Chinese official records of the year 166 contain this note:

"Men from the kingdom of An-tun arrived at our capital with presents. . . . From that time direct intercourse with this kingdom began."(1) (See Source List, p. 168.)

What kingdom was it? "An-tun" undoubtedly means the Roman Emperor, Marcus Aurelius *Anton*-inus. Already for 200 years Roman merchants had looked to China for one luxury which wealthy women demanded, silk. At that time only the Chinese had silkworms, and the thread or cloth was carried overland, across deserts and mountains to Indian ports. The Chinese record refers to a group of Roman merchants, trying to arrange a more direct trade.

We began with Origen's words about Roman peace and communications in the purposes of God. By the year 166 those communications stretched over three continents. The time had come.

GREEK LANGUAGE AND GREEK THOUGHT

The men whom Christ commissioned to go as His witnesses "to the end of the earth" were Jews. They did not need to learn languages of this country and that country before they could go. The spoken language of Jews in Palestine was Aramaic, but most of them also spoke some Greek. Greek had become the most-used language all round the east end of the Mediterranean. In Mesopotamia, and further east, almost everywhere some people spoke and read Greek. Latin was the main language in Italy, but St Paul used Greek even when he wrote his letter to the Church in Rome. In that letter he wrote, "I hope to see you in passing as I go to Spain" (Rom. 15.24). Even as far west as Spain he would find Greek-speaking merchants.

Few of the missionaries had so many advantages as Paul. The Roman officer who arrested Paul after the riot in Jerusalem (Acts 21.33) must

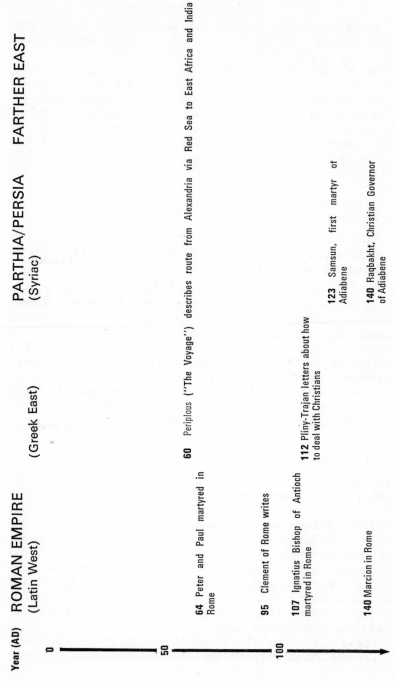

Year (AD)

ROMAN EMPIRE
(Latin West)

(Greek East)

PARTHIA/PERSIA   FARTHER EAST
(Syriac)

0

50

60 Periplous ("The Voyage") describes route from Alexandria via Red Sea to East Africa and India

64 Peter and Paul martyred in Rome

95 Clement of Rome writes

100

107 Ignatius Bishop of Antioch martyred in Rome

112 Pliny-Trajan letters about how to deal with Christians

123 Samsun, first martyr of Adiabene

140 Marcion in Rome

140 Raqbakht, Christian Governor of Adiabene

8

Year (AD)	ROMAN EMPIRE (Latin West)	(Greek East)	PARTHIA/PERSIA (Syriac)	FARTHER EAST
150			**150** Tatian the "Syrian" converted at Rome	
		156 Polycarp martyred at Smyrna. Montanus teaching in Asia Minor		
	165 Justin martyred in Rome			**166** Chinese record of embassy from Roman Empire
		175 Celsus, anti-Christian writer		
	177 Irenaeus Bishop of Lyons			
		180 Clement head of College at Alexandria	**180** Abgar VIII of Edessa, first Christian king	**180** Pantaenus of Alexandria, missionary to India
	195 Tertullian of Carthage converted			
200			**200** Bardaisan teaching in Edessa	
		202 Origen head of College at Alexandria		
			224 Persian Empire revives under Sassanid Dynasty	
		231 Origen moves to Caesarea in Palestine		
		240 Gregory the "Wonderworker" in Pontus		
250		**250** Emperor Decius persecutes Christians		
	258 Cyprian martyred in Carthage	**261** Emperor Gallienus tolerates Christians		
		271 Antony, the "model for monks"		
			294 Gregory the "Enlightener" first Bishop of Armenia	

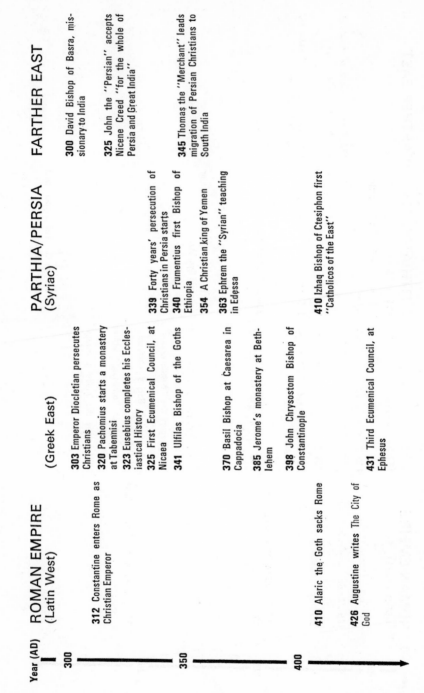

FARTHER EAST

300 David Bishop of Basra, missionary to India

325 John the "Persian" accepts Nicene Creed "for the whole of Persia and Great India"

345 Thomas the "Merchant" leads migration of Persian Christians to South India

PARTHIA/PERSIA
(Syriac)

339 Forty years' persecution of Christians in Persia starts

340 Frumentius first Bishop of Ethiopia

354 A Christian king of Yemen

363 Ephrem the "Syrian" teaching in Edessa

410 Izhaq Bishop of Ctesiphon first "Catholicos of the East"

ROMAN EMPIRE
(Greek East)

303 Emperor Diocletian persecutes Christians

320 Pachomius starts a monastery at Tabennisi

323 Eusebius completes his Ecclesiastical History

325 First Ecumenical Council, at Nicaea

341 Ulfilas Bishop of the Goths

370 Basil Bishop at Caesarea in Cappadocia

385 Jerome's monastery at Bethlehem

398 John Chrysostom Bishop of Constantinople

431 Third Ecumenical Council, at Ephesus

ROMAN EMPIRE
(Latin West)

312 Constantine enters Rome as Christian Emperor

410 Alaric the Goth sacks Rome

426 Augustine writes The City of God

Year (AD)

300

350

400

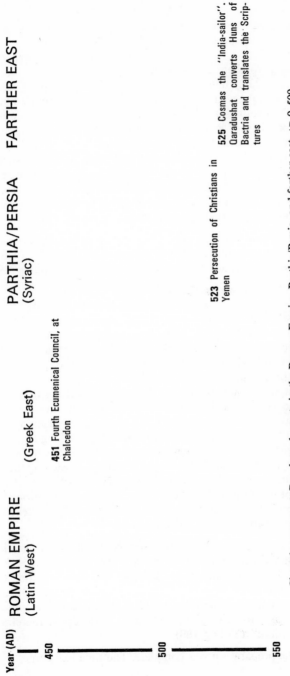

Year (AD)   ROMAN EMPIRE
(Latin West)

(Greek East)

PARTHIA/PERSIA
(Syriac)

FARTHER EAST

451 Fourth Ecumenical Council, at Chalcedon

523 Persecution of Christians in Yemen

525 Cosmas the "India-sailor". Qaradushat converts Huns of Bactria and translates the Scriptures

Chart 1: TIME LINE: People and events in the Roman Empire, Parthia/Persia, and farther east, AD 0–500

11

have felt that there were three Pauls, not one. First, Paul spoke to the officer in Greek, and told him that he belonged to Tarsus, a city with a Greek university (Acts 21.37–39). Second, Paul quietened the crowd by speaking to them in their own "Hebrew language", i.e. Aramaic (Acts 21.40—22.2), telling of his further Hebrew education in Jerusalem. And third, Paul gave the officer a fright (for he had allowed his soldiers to treat Paul roughly) by claiming that he, Paul, was of a family which had the privilege of Roman citizenship (22.25–29). Paul belonged to all three spheres, Greek, Hebrew, and Roman.

Some of the other Apostles could not speak or write Greek so well. A bishop named Papias (about 130) tells us that Peter used Mark as interpreter. Some scholars think that Mark may have interpreted into Latin, but in any case the young city man would have spoken Greek better than the fisherman. Papias says:

> "Mark wrote down carefully, but not in order of time, all that he remembered about what Christ had said and done. . . . His one aim was not to leave out or to mis-state anything." (Young **209**)

That was how the earliest Gospel came to be written.

All the documents, which were later brought together to form the New Testament, were in Greek. Three centuries before, Jews of Alexandria had translated their Hebrew Scriptures (our Old Testament) from Hebrew into Greek. So the whole of what is now our Bible was available in this widely-used language. This helped to speed the Christian message on its way.

All languages have words for things which belong to everyday life, but some languages do not have words for any deep thought. The Greeks were used to discussing ideas, morals, the meaning of life, the nature of God. They had words for everything, a language richer than any language before. Thought cannot go forward without words to express it, but a rich language makes possible far-reaching thought. This Greek contribution was recognized by early Christian thinkers. Of the Roman peace, Origen said, "God was preparing the nations". We may now quote Clement of Alexandria, who was Origen's teacher, about God's preparation among the Greeks:

> "God is the cause of all good things, some directly, others indirectly. He is the direct cause of Old and New Testaments. He is the indirect cause of Greek Philosophy. Perhaps we may say that God gave Philosophy to the Greeks, till the Lord should call the Greeks. For as the Law educated the Hebrews (Gal. 3.24), so Philosophy educated the Greeks, to bring them to Christ. Philosophy, therefore, was a preparation." (Young **100**)

Again, the preparation was complete. The time had come.

HEBREW RELIGION

The greatest preparation for the coming of Christ was in Hebrew religion. We cannot do better than turn to Origen again, and to words which he wrote in answer to Celsus's sneer at Christianity's origin being in so small a corner of the world (see p. 1):

"God has not been asleep. Every good thing which ever happened among men has been the work of God. But Christ's coming could only be to a place, where men believed that God is one; where men were reading the Prophets who point to Christ; and where men were learning that Christ should come at a time when, from this one place, His teaching would overflow into all the world." (See Young **1**)

From Origen's statement, we will examine two points:

1. the Scriptures of the Jews pointed to Christ,
2. the religion of the Jews was preparing the world for Christ's teaching.

THE SCRIPTURES OF THE JEWS POINTED TO CHRIST

According to all the Gospels, Jesus claimed to be the fulfilment of prophecy. In the synagogue at Nazareth, after reading Isaiah 61.1–2, he closed the book and said, "Today this scripture has been fulfilled in your hearing" (Luke 4.21). His entering Jerusalem riding on a donkey (Matt. 21.2–5) was a detailed fulfilment of Zechariah 9.9. On the road to Emmaus, "beginning with Moses and all the Prophets, he interpreted to them in all the scriptures the things concerning himself" (Luke 24.27).

Missionary preachers and teachers, as recorded in Acts and Epistles, continued to make this claim that the promised Saviour had come.

Justin, a missionary in Rome about 140, told his readers to look for:
"the best and truest evidence, in the books of the Prophets, where we find announced one born of a Virgin; healing the sick and raising the dead; being hated, disowned, and crucified; dying, rising again, and ascending to heaven." (Young **103**)

Justin was a Greek who, after long searching for true religion, believed that he was finding it in the teaching of Plato. Then, at Ephesus, an old man told him of "men, more ancient than those who are called philosophers". He introduced him to the Old Testament Prophets, and to Christ who is their fulfilment. Justin continues:

"As for me, a fire was kindled in my soul, and I was held fast by love for the Prophets, and for those men who are the friends of Christ" (i.e. the Apostles). (Young **76**)

Having himself come to be a Christian in that way, that was how Justin tried to win others to the Faith, both heathen, as he had been, and Jews

1.2 "Greek had become the most-used language . . . 'Philosophy educated Greeks, to bring them to Christ.' " (pp. 7, 12)
Carving on a sarcophagus (stone coffin) shows two philosophers holding scrolls, and a pupil.

1.3 "Christ's coming could only be to a place . . . where men were reading the prophets who point to Christ." (p. 13) A fresco discovered in the synagogue at Dura-Europos shows the prophet Ezra as a teacher reading the Hebrew Scriptures. Some of the Jews and adherents who worshipped there may have joined the house-church at Dura.

as well. He boldly told the Jews, "These Scriptures are more ours than yours", meaning, "You Jews have the prophecies, but we Christians have the fulfilment."

Here is a good sample of Justin's teaching:

"The Prophet says,

'Out of Zion shall go forth the law,
and the word of the Lord from Jerusalem.
. . . Nation shall not lift up sword against nation,
neither shall they learn war any more' (Isa. 2.3, 4).

And from Jerusalem there *did* go out, men twelve in number, unlearned, with no ability in speech. In the power of God they preached to every race of men . . . and we, who formerly used to kill one another, now not only do not make war against our enemies, but are willing to die for confessing Christ." (Young **6**)

Christian preachers felt the need of "scriptural authority", the need to be able to say, "Our message must be true, because it is in this ancient holy Book." The writings which we call "New Testament" were *so* new that non-Christians did not know or respect them. Preachers, however, could follow the example of Christ Himself and appeal to "the words which the Prophets have spoken".

THE RELIGION OF THE JEWS WAS
PREPARING THE WORLD FOR CHRIST'S TEACHING

At the time of Christ, Jews living outside Palestine numbered several times as many as those living in Palestine. The Greek geographer Strabo (AD 7) wrote:

"Jews have gone into every city, and it is hard to find a place on earth which has not admitted them, and come under their control." (2)

The suggestion that Jews had "control" is an exaggeration. The Jews had no political power, but they were capable businessmen, with a high standard of education and a still higher standard of religion.

Jews were to be found from Spain in the west right across Europe and western Asia to Persia and Arabia (see maps 3 and 4), and perhaps in India too. Jewish communities on the west coast of India today claim to be so long established. In Africa, Jews lived at many places on the north coast; there were perhaps a million in Egypt and many far up the Nile valley and in Ethiopia (map 5).

Every Jewish community had its synagogue and school, worship and instruction on the Sabbath (Saturday), and prayers every day. So the religion of this small nation became widely known.

Many non-Jews were dissatisfied with their own religions, and no longer believed the old stories of gods who were lustful and violent like the worst of men. There were teachers—especially Greek philosophers —who taught about *one* God who is above all others, good, beautiful, and true. Often a man who had begun to accept such ideas wondered, "Where can I find the regular worship of the one true God, further instruction about Him, and a fellowship with others who believe in Him?"

One obvious answer was: "At the synagogue", so he would come and ask, "May I be allowed to attend on the Sabbath?" Jews of an earlier time would have said, "No. Only a man born of Jewish parents can belong to the People of God." But one of the later Prophets had seen God's greater purpose for His People, who had been purified by the sufferings of exile in Babylonia:

"I (God) will give you as a light to the nations, that my salvation may reach to the end of the earth" (Isa. 49.6).

So there had come to be a recognized place in the synagogue for non-Jews who believed in God and led worthy lives. We should call them "adherents". In the New Testament they are called "men that fear God" (see Acts 13.16).

There had also come to be recognized a way by which an adherent might become (as we should say today) a full member. The word used in the New Testament for a non-Jewish convert to Judaism is "proselyte", see Acts 2.10. To become a member, a man must (a) make an offering, (b) undergo a ceremony of washing, called "the bath of purity" (which is connected with the origin of Christian baptism, p. 23), and (c) obey the Law of Moses, i.e. be circumcised, and ever afterwards keep the Jewish rules about "clean" and "unclean" food. This third item was the biggest demand. A man had to leave the customs of Gentile society, and really become a Jew. Many sincere believers could not bring themselves to do that. So they remained "adherents", a little Gentile group at the back of the synagogue's congregation, continuing as friends of the Jewish community, but never coming to belong.

The Acts of the Apostles includes many stories of Christian missionaries who won such Gentile adherents as their converts. The first of these stories is about a man of Africa. Philip baptized him at the roadside, as he was returning from Jerusalem to Meroe, 1,700 miles up the Nile Valley (Acts 8.26–39). Then Peter baptized an army officer at the Roman headquarters for Palestine, Caesarea (Acts 10). Both had been adherents of the synagogue before they became members of the Church.

In many towns, Paul began by preaching in the synagogue, with startling results among Gentile adherents. At Pisidian Antioch his message was that it is faith in Christ, rather than keeping the Law of Moses, which sets a man right with God. "When the Gentiles heard this, they were glad . . . and many believed" (Acts 13.48). At Corinth such preaching set the synagogue in uproar. Paul walked out, and Titius Justus, a Gentile adherent, opened his house next door. There Paul was joined by the ruler of the synagogue himself and all his family. "And many of the Corinthians, hearing Paul (there) believed, and were baptized". (See Acts 18.4–8.) Thus next door to the synagogue was a house which on Sunday was the Christians' church.

People who had looked to the synagogue, now entered the Church. We shall see this continuing in the work of later missionaries, and over a much wider area. Hebrew religion had prepared the way.

STUDY SUGGESTIONS

1. For what reason has the geographical situation of Palestine always been a dangerous one?
2. Name the continents in which each of the following "Powers" are or were situated:
   (a) Babylon (b) Egypt) (c) Greece (d) Rome
3. (a) For what reason was Palestine a suitable place for the start of a religion that was to spread "into all the world"?
   (b) In what three chief ways did the early Christians see that God had prepared for the coming of Christianity?
4. Read the following passages and say in each case:
   (i)   Who was travelling,
   (ii) Where they were going,
   (iii) By what method you think they may have travelled.
   (a) Matt. 21.1–11   (b) Acts 8.26–31   (c) Acts 9.1–8
   Which if any of these methods of travel are used in your own country today?
5. (a) Name three kinds of "luxury goods" which a merchant of Alexandria might have imported from Asia in the first century AD.
   (b) If these goods are available in your country today, find out where they come from.
6. (a) Why was it not necessary for Jewish Christians in the first century to learn the languages of countries to which they were sent as missionaries?
   (b) What advantages did Paul have over other Christian missionaries of his time?
   (c) For what two reasons was Greek a useful language for the spreading of the Christian Gospel?
   (d) Which modern language do you think is the most useful for spreading the Gospel today? Give your reasons.
7. (a) Who was Origen? When did he live, and what important work did he do for the Church?

(b) What reply did Origen make to Celsus's remark that Palestine was too small a "corner" to be the birthplace of God's Son?

8. Who was Justin and how did he come to be a Christian?

9. In what way did early Christian missionaries and preachers use the Jewish Scriptures to support their message?

10. Read the following passages, and in each case:
    (i) Name the prophet or prophets whose words were quoted,
    (ii) Say briefly what he or they had prophesied about the coming of Christ.
    (a) Matt. 4.12–16 (b) Matt. 8.14–17 (c) Matt. 12.15–21
    (d) Luke 4.16–19 (e) Luke 24.44–47 (f) Rom. 9.22–26
    (g) Acts 2.16–21

11. Give:
    (a) One or two reasons why people (non-Jews) in the Roman Empire became dissatisfied with their pagan religions;
    (b) One or two reasons why some pagans became converts to Judaism;
    (c) One or two reasons why some pagans were *un*willing to become "full members" of the Jewish religion;
    (d) One or two reasons why some pagans were more willing to accept the Christian faith than they were to accept Judaism.

12. Who or what were the following?
    The *Periplous* Pantaenus adherents

CHAPTER 2

The House-Church

WHOSE HOUSE, AND WHERE?

Three great events in the early history of Christianity took place in a Jerusalem house: the Lord's supper (Mark 14.12–26), the appearances of Jesus to the Apostles after His Resurrection (John 20.14–29), and the coming of the Holy Spirit (Acts 2). These events are so important that we must want to know all that can be known about that house. Let us do some detective work upon it.

First, do we know that all three passages refer to the *same* house? Mark describes it as having a guest-room (Mark 14.14), large and upstairs (v. 15), for Jesus and His Apostles. According to Acts 1, after the Ascension, the Apostles "returned . . . and went up to the upper room where they were staying" (Acts 1.12, 13). And it seems that it was a very big room, because 120 people gathered with the Apostles there (v. 15). Acts 2 begins with the Twelve "all together in one place". No change of place is mentioned, so we assume that the "place" was the same as in Acts 1. John merely says, "the doors being shut where the disciples were" (John 20.19), which seems to mean (as in Acts 1.12) "where they were staying". So the three passages probably do refer to the same house. Can we find out anything more about it?

A Jerusalem house where many Christians gathered for prayer is mentioned in Acts 12. Peter, strangely escaped from Herod's prison, knew where he would find his friends. The servant girl at the gate, Rhoda, knew his voice, so he must have been a frequent visitor. She was so glad that she ran into the house to tell the others, leaving Peter shut outside. This is one of Luke's vivid stories. Perhaps Luke mentions the girl's name because he got the story from Rhoda herself. We know the name, not only of the servant, but of her mistress. This was "the house of Mary the mother of John, whose other name was Mark"—the Mark who later wrote the earliest of the Gospels. Could this again be the same house?

One more clue may persuade us that it *was* the same house. When Mark wrote of the arrest of Jesus in the garden called Gethsemane, he included an incident which Matthew and Luke left out. When the others ran away,

"a young man followed Jesus, with nothing but a linen cloth (sheet) about his body; and they seized him, but he left the linen cloth, and ran away naked" (Mark 14.51).

19

If the house with the upstairs guest-room was the house of Mary the mother of Mark, perhaps this was young Mark himself. When, after supper, Jesus and His friends went out, Mark heard them, got up from bed, and followed without waiting to dress. He may have remembered the incident with mixed feelings. Perhaps he was proud to have had even this small part in these great events. Perhaps he was ashamed to tell of the faint-heartedness of others—"they all forsook him and fled"—without adding the story of his own faint-heartedness.

Our detective work has led us to the house of Mary the mother of Mark in Jerusalem, as being probably the place of meeting for the first congregation of Christ's Church, the first of the "house-churches".

Other house-churches are mentioned in the New Testament, with the names of the people in whose houses they met, e.g. at Philippi (Acts 16.40), Corinth (Acts 18.7), Rome (Rom. 16.5; 16.14; 16.15), Ephesus (1 Cor. 16.19), Laodicea (Col. 4.15), Colossae (Philemon 1 and 2) (see p. 95). Such phrases as "the brethren who are with them", "the saints" (i.e. fellow Christians) "who are with them" seem to mean "who are in their house-church". Several of these house-churches, like the one in Jerusalem, were in the homes of women, probably widows. In some cases both husband and wife are named. Where other names are added, they probably represent grown-up members of the family. In one house-church only men are mentioned.

House-churches such as these were the only churches that Christians had, not only throughout the New Testament period, but through most of the second century. One report says that a church building was set up at Arbil, east of the river Tigris, before 148 (see p. 95 and map 4). There is more evidence that there was a church building in Edessa, 300 miles west of Arbil, sometime after 180 when the King of Edessa became a Christian. The building was destroyed by flood in 201 (see p. 85).

Christians in the Roman Empire were content to continue meeting in houses. Other religions had their temples; Jews had their synagogues; but Christians were something new. They were not recognized by the government and were often suspected, always insecure. In some places Christians did own land for the graves of their dead. It was customary in the Empire for people to club together in order to secure land for graves, and one such "burial society" composed of Christians would not be specially noticed. In this period, graves were the Church's only property.

About 250, we hear of a few churches being built, where Christians were most numerous, in Pontus (see map 3, p. 43), Asia Minor, Syria, and Egypt. But in that very year, 250, came persecution, which was Empire-wide, and the Christians lost their buildings (see p. 74).

At Dura-Europos, a Roman frontier fortress (see map 4), one house-church building has actually survived and may be visited today. Archaeologists discovered it under the sand in 1934. The house was built before AD 100. We do not know when Christians first used it as their meeting place, but in 232 the building was altered and made more suitable for services. One inner wall was taken down, and so two rooms became one larger meeting room, and in it a platform was built for the altar. In a smaller room stands a shallow stone bath. Anyone to be baptized stood there, while water was poured over him. There were paintings on the baptistry walls, and enough paint remains for us to recognize the subjects, and see what baptism meant to those Christians seventeen centuries ago. The central picture shows the Good Shepherd bringing a sheep to the flock (John 10.14–16). On the side walls are the healed paralytic (Mark 2.5: "Your sins are forgiven"), Jesus taking Peter from the water into the boat (Matt. 14.31: the boat represents the Church), the woman with her water-pot at Jacob's well (John 4.10: "living water"), and the three women at the empty tomb (Mark 16 and Rom. 6.4: "As Christ was raised, we too . . . walk in newness of life").

WHAT HAPPENED IN THE HOUSE-CHURCH?

What did Christians do in these house-churches, most of which were just ordinary house buildings? Vivid descriptions have come down to us, of a preacher at Smyrna for example, of the Eucharist in Rome, of Baptism in Carthage, and so on. We must not think that Christians did things in the same way everywhere. But as we mention one place and another we shall be seeing real scenes, meeting real people, and catching something of the spirit of these house-churches. We must also be careful not to imagine the Early Church as altogether good. These samples which we shall look at now are good ones, but in later chapters of this book we shall come upon problems, failures, mistakes, divisions. As Christ Himself said, there were "weeds among the wheat" (Matt. 13.25).

One of the best sources of information is Justin (see pp. 13ff), who, about 155, wrote to explain Christian ways to non-Christians. We shall take his accounts of (1) Baptism, (2) Sunday worship, (3) preaching, (4) Eucharist. We shall add other source material on some of these subjects, and also on (5) Church discipline, (6) the Church and those in need, (7) death and burial, (8) teaching on how to say one's prayers. Finally we shall consider (9) Easter, Pentecost, Epiphany, and Christmas.

BAPTISM
Justin begins where the Christian life begins:

"We tell those who accept Christian teaching, and promise to live the Christian life, to pray and fast for forgiveness, we ourselves praying

2.1 and 2.2. In baptism "We bring them where there is water." (p. 23)
Early Christians used many different ideas to symbolize baptism. Sometimes they remembered the story of Jesus opening the eyes of the blind, as on the 4th-century sarcophagus of Sabinus, or sometimes deer drinking at a fountain (especially when Psalm 23 was used in the service), as in a mosaic at Carthage.

2.3 In prayer "the best position is to stand with your hands held out." (p. 30)
This attitude was customary among early Christians, as many frescoes in the catacombs, and this figure on a sarcophagus, show.

and fasting with them. We then bring them where there is water, and they are born again, just as all we Christians have been. Washed in the name of the Father, Son and Holy Spirit . . . as we learned from the Apostles. . . .

We then bring them to the place where the other Christians are assembled. We all pray, for ourselves, for the newly baptized, and for others everywhere, asking God that, as we have learned the truth, we may now show by our deeds that we are good citizens and keepers of the commandments, and so we may be saved with eternal salvation. After the prayers we greet each other as brothers." (Young 117)

Justin then goes on to describe the Eucharist (see below) for the newly-baptized, explaining that no one is admitted except believers who have been baptized, and who live as Christ has taught. Justin ends this part of his account with these words:

"After these services we always keep reminding one another of them, and those who have, come to the help of those in need, and we always keep together." (See also Young 133)

Tertullian, a Roman lawyer born in Carthage in north Africa (map 3), became a Christian in 195 (see p. 27). As a lawyer he had learned to choose vivid and persuasive words. He returned to Carthage and used this skill as a Christian teacher, presbyter, and writer. Tertullian always has something to say which makes the hearer listen, and think, and remember. For example, this about baptism:

"It is all so simple—no great show, nothing new, no expense. A man is dipped in water, and a few words are said. He comes out of the water, not much (if any) the cleaner. Is it not wonderful that death is washed away by bathing? . . . We too wonder, but we wonder because we believe." (3)

Tertullian also mentions the Greek word *Ichthus*, meaning "Fish". It was widely used as a sign among Christians, because its five Greek letters (both *ch* and *th* are single letters in Greek) could be made to represent five words:

LETTER	GREEK WORD, IN ROMAN LETTERS	TRANSLATED INTO ENGLISH
I	Iesous	Jesus
Ch	Christos	Christ
Th	Theou	God's
U	Uios	Son
S	Soter	Saviour

The fish sign is to be found on ancient Christian rings, seals, ornaments, and gravestones. Tertullian thinks of this sign in writing about baptism:

"We Christians are little fishes, and, like our *Ichthus* (i.e. Jesus Christ, God's Son, Saviour) are born in the water. The way to kill little fishes is to take them out of the water." (4)

Tertullian means that, if a Christian forgets his baptism, that is the end of him.

Sometimes the sign of the fish stands, not for Christ and the water of baptism (as here), but for Christ as the Christians' spiritual food, at the Eucharist.

SUNDAY WORSHIP

Justin describes the worship in house-churches:

"On the day called Sunday, there is a meeting for all in one place, according to the city or countryside where one lives.

The Memoirs of the Apostles (i.e. the Gospels), or the writings of the Prophets, are read as long as there is time. When the reader has finished, the President, in a sermon, calls us to imitate these good things.

Then we all stand and pray." (Young **133**)

Justin calls the leader of the worship "president" because non-Christians might not understand special words such as "bishop" or "presbyter".

The three items mentioned: reading of Scripture, a sermon based on the reading, and prayers (which were said standing), follow the custom of the synagogue. Justin names the New Testament lesson as being from the Gospels (and puts this first), and the Old Testament lesson as an alternative, from the Prophets. This reminds us that it was through reading the Prophets and finding Christ as their fulfilment, that Justin became a Christian (see pp. 13, 14).

PREACHING

We may add to Justin's mention of the sermon some words of Irenaeus. Irenaeus, who was Bishop of Lyons in Gaul (now France, map 3) from 177 to 200, wrote about the preaching of an aged Bishop, Polycarp, in the house-church at Smyrna. Irenaeus in his boyhood had heard Polycarp preach, and this preaching made a lasting impression upon him:

"Lessons received as a boy, make an impression which becomes part of the mind, and the impression remains, growing as the mind grows. So I can tell the very place where the blessed Polycarp, sitting down, used to preach; his comings out and goings in; his bodily appearance; and the talks which he used to make for the congregation. He used to talk of his going about with John, and with the others who had seen the Lord, about their sayings, this and that which he had heard from them about the Lord, about his mighty acts and his teaching.

And because Polycarp had received it from eye-witnesses of the Word of life, Polycarp used to tell everything just as it is in the Scriptures.

Even then, the mercy of God was upon me, and I used to listen eagerly, noting these things, not on paper, but in my heart." (Young **128**)

Note that in the house-church the preacher *sat*, as Christ did in the synagogue at Nazareth (Luke 4.20, 21). This is Jewish custom still. The "comings out and goings in" were probably from some side-room of the house, and back again after service.

Such preaching as that of Polycarp could never happen again. When Irenaeus wrote, about the year 180, no preacher was left alive who had been taught by an Apostle who had actually known Jesus. But we should note what Irenaeus has said: that which Polycarp received from the eye-witnesses was "just as it is in the Scriptures". The New Testament *is* what the eye-witnesses passed on. So our preaching today can have the same basis that Polycarp's preaching had.

EUCHARIST

Justin describes the Eucharist, which, after the service of Scripture reading, preaching, and prayers, was the crown of Sunday's worship:

"Bread is brought to the President, and wine mixed with water. He says a prayer of thanksgiving, as well as he is able, and the congregation say *Amen*, which is Hebrew for 'May it be so'. The deacons give the bread and wine to all present, and take it to those absent.

Those who are well off, and who want to do so, give to the collection. This is placed with the President, and he takes care of orphans, widows, and those ill or otherwise in need, those in prison, and strangers who are staying here. In fact, he becomes the helper of all who are in need." (Young **133**)

(See *The Church and those in need*, pp. 27, 28.)

Justin continues:

"Only believers, who have received the washing of forgiveness and of rebirth, and who live as Christ has taught, can receive this food (the bread and wine) which is called Eucharist. For it is to us, not just bread and wine. Jesus Christ became flesh and blood to save us. And we are taught that this food, blessed by prayer of words from Him, is the flesh and blood of Jesus, who became flesh." (Young **134**)

Some of Justin's words need explanation:

Eucharist. Justin says the food is called eucharist, but he means the

2.4. and 2.5 "Only believers can receive this food which is called Eucharist." (p. 25)
The fresco of a Eucharistic meal, in the catacomb of Calixtus in Rome, dates from
before AD 313.

A later mosaic illustrating the Last Supper, in the Church of St Apollinaris at
Ravenna, shows the kind of table and cloth used for the Eucharist, and its customary
decoration, in the late 5th and early 6th centuries.

whole service. *Eucharistia* is Greek for "thanksgiving". Christ began, as the celebrant begins, by giving thanks (1 Cor. 11.24).

Wine mixed with water. At the time of Christ, poorer people added water to their wine at meal times, as many people in Mediterranean countries still do today. So probably this was done at the first Lord's Supper.

As well as he is able. Evidently the prayer of thanksgiving, or Eucharistic Prayer, was not yet in one set form, except for "the prayer of words from Him" (see below).

Blessed by prayer. A literal translation would be "eucharisted", a new Christian word.

Of Words from Him (Christ). The words of institution from 1 Cor. 11.23–25. Justin goes on to quote them. All down the centuries, and across the world, these words are central in the Eucharist.

Not just bread and wine. Irenaeus, Bishop of Lyons (see p. 24), wrote similarly of Christ's presence in the Eucharist.

"We offer to God things which are His. . . . Bread comes from the earth, but, offered to God, it is no longer just bread. It now is something heavenly, as well as earthly. So our bodies, which will die, receiving the Eucharist, have the hope of resurrection to life eternal." (Young **135**)

Both statements are based on Scripture. Justin was recalling Christ's words, "This is my body . . . This is my blood". Irenaeus was recalling, "I am the bread of life" (John 6.35). A collection for the poor continues to be a part of the service in most Churches. Compare what Tertullian says (below) about a monthly collection.

CHURCH DISCIPLINE

This is what Tertullian of Carthage says about discipline of Church members, and about those who conduct it:

"Church discipline is conducted gravely, since we know that we act in God's sight, especially gravely when, because of serious sin, someone has to be put out of our fellowship.

Our presbyters preside over us, appointed not because of money paid, but because of proved character. There is no buying and selling of the things of God." (Abbreviated from Young **136**)

THE CHURCH AND THOSE IN NEED

Tertullian, as quoted above, continues:

"We do have our money-box, contributed to by those who wish, and who are able, once a month. The money is used, not for feasting and drinking, but to help the poor, orphaned children, the old, the shipwrecked, Christians sent to forced-labour in the mines, or exiled to islands, or shut up in prison. This is why people say of us, 'See, how these Christians love one another!'" (Young **177**)

Tertullian wrote this in Carthage, about 197. It may be compared with what Justin had written earlier in Rome about the collection for the poor and its uses (see p. 25).

About the year 250, the Churches in Rome, besides supporting their bishop, 46 presbyters, and a large number of lesser officers from readers to doorkeepers, had (according to Eusebius)

"more than 1,500 widows and poor people, all kept by the grace and loving care of the Master" (Christ). (Young **41**)

Later again, in 362, the anti-Christian Roman Emperor, Julian, complained:

"The Christians feed not only their own poor, but ours as well, while no one in need looks to the temples." (Young **179**)

He might truly have said that people in need did not look to the State either. The Church was far ahead of the State in social concern and in social service.

DEATH AND BURIAL

We saw earlier that graves were at first the Church's only property. Grave-stones provide the earliest Christian sculpture. The favourite figure to be found on them is that of the Good Shepherd, bringing home the sheep on his shoulders.

Here is a Christian description of funerals, written by Aristides, an Athenian (map 3), about 140:

"If any righteous person among us passes away from this world, we rejoice and give thanks to God, and follow his body as if he were moving from one place to another." (Young **181**)

Perpetua, a young woman of Carthage who was in prison and soon to be martyred, in the year 202 described her dream about death:

"I saw a huge garden, and in the middle of it a tall man with white hair, dressed like a shepherd . . . and around him many thousands dressed in white. He raised his hand, looked at me, and said, 'It is good that you have come, my child'. . . . He gave me food, which I received on hands laid one upon another, and everyone said 'Amen'. I awoke, with the sweet taste still in my mouth." (5)

This was the way in which the bread of the Eucharist was received.

2.6–8 "Christians have the commandments of Christ written on their hearts. They acknowledge the goodness of God to them." (p. 49)

Christians in the early centuries also liked to acknowledge their faith by putting Christian symbols on everyday objects, as here on a ring, seal, and ceremonial bowl.

TEACHING ON HOW TO PRAY

One of the best examples of such teaching comes from Origen. It was written at Caesarea (map 3) about the year 236. This short summary of one part of his book keeps as closely as possible to his own words:

> *How to pray:* Settle your mind. Put yourself in God's presence and act as though God was there, looking at you. Then you will hear the Lord's reply, "Here I am" (Isa. 58.9). This is the greatest answer to prayer, to know the presence of God.
>
> You do not pray alone. Christ prays with you, and the angels, who rejoice over one sinner who turns to God, pray with you.
>
> *When to pray:* We are told to pray always, because the good life is a prayer. Prayer, in the ordinary sense, should be at least three times each day (Dan. 6.10): morning (Ps. 5.3), noon (Acts 10.9), and evening (Ps. 141.2).
>
> *What to pray for:* Pray for yourselves, pray for others, and give thanks. Remember to ask for the greatest things (Matt. 6.33).
>
> *Stand, kneel, or sit?* The best position is to stand, with hands held out, and eyes looking up, even as you want to lift up your soul, and raise your mind to God. (See picture, p. 22.)
>
> Kneeling is right, when you are asking God's forgiveness. But you may pray sitting, e.g. if your feet ache; or even lying down, if you have a fever.
>
> Sometimes, e.g. at sea, or in a crowd, you must not bother about position at all.
>
> *Place of prayer:* Any place can be the right place. A place becomes the right place when you pray in it. In your own home, choose a quiet place, clean and good, which can be made your holy place. There is one place where we most expect the presence of angels, the power of the Lord himself, the spirits of holy men—both those still living, and those passed on. I mean the place where the congregation of the faithful meets. (See Young **173**)

THE CHRISTIAN FESTIVALS:
EASTER, PENTECOST, EPIPHANY, CHRISTMAS

Justin used the name "Sunday" for the day for Christians to worship together. This name, "Day of the Sun", came from nature worship, but it was easy to link with Christian ideas. Christ is the "Sun of righteousness" (Mal. 4.2), and "the Light of the world" (John 9.5). Justin also thought of Sunday as the first day of Creation, when God said, "Let there be light", and the day when Jesus rose from the dead. In the New Testament we can see that for Christians this day was already beginning to take the place of the Sabbath (Saturday) of the Jews (Acts 20.7; 1 Cor. 16.2; Rev. 1.10). This last Scripture reference gives the day its true name, the Lord's Day.

Strict Jews fasted twice in the week (Luke 18.12), on Monday and Thursday. By the year 100, Christians also fasted twice, but had changed the days to Wednesday and Friday. On Wednesday they remembered the Betrayal of Jesus (Mark 14.10), and on Friday His Crucifixion (Mark 15.24, 25).

But these events happened, not only on certain days of the week, but at a special time of the year, about the time of the Jewish Passover on the "14th of the month Nisan", which means the first full moon in spring. This is the festival which commemorates the escape of the Israelites from slavery in Egypt. So Christians in Asia Minor celebrated Easter on the same day as the Jewish Passover. For Jews, the Passover is a time for family gatherings. They wish each other "a happy Passover", as Christians wish "a merry Christmas". Christians, however, began their "14th Nisan" with a solemn fast, remembering the Crucifixion, and ended that same day with joyful Eucharist, remembering the Resurrection.

This custom was unknown in the west, when Polycarp, Bishop of Smyrna (see p. 24), visited Rome in 154 and tried to persuade the Bishop of Rome that it was a custom handed down by the Apostles. A little later we find Easter being observed in Alexandria and in Rome on the *Sunday following* the Jewish Passover. It was observed on Sunday because that day of the week was the Resurrection Day, and it seemed wrong that the yearly festival should be on any other day but Sunday. So Easter, Christianity's oldest and greatest festival, came to be fixed for the first Sunday after the spring full moon, with the previous Friday (now called Good Friday) as the fast commemorating the Crucifixion.

The fast before the Easter festival was gradually lengthened from two days, Friday and Saturday, to a whole week, and then to forty days, now called Lent in English. Easter was the favourite time for converts to come to be baptized, so the forty days were used as the time of preparation.

Because the Holy Spirit came to the disciples on the Jewish Pentecost (a harvest festival, the name being Greek for "fiftieth", i e. the fiftieth day after Passover), Christians fixed their celebration of the coming of the Holy Spirit on the fiftieth day, i.e. the seventh Sunday, after Easter.

The festival of the Ascension was held in between, forty days after Easter (Acts 1.3). Pentecost became the second great Christian festival. In English it came to be called Whit (i.e. white) Sunday, because, as at Easter, there were so many newly baptized at that time and they were dressed in white.

By the fourth century, two more great festivals were added, Epiphany (6 January), and Christmas (25 December). No one knew Christ's real birthday, but in many parts of the northern hemisphere there had been ancient festivals of rejoicing in late December or early January, at the passing of the shortest day. The winter festival of the Romans was called "the festival of the Unconquered Sun".

By this time Helena, the mother of the pro-Christian Roman Emperor Constantine (p. 81), had built the Church of the Nativity over the Bethlehem cave where Jesus was born. To this church, Bishop and people came in midnight procession on 6 January each year to celebrate His *Epiphany* (Greek for "appearing"). This festival was also connected with Christ's baptism; when He "appeared" as God's beloved Son.

The Armenian Church (see p. 89) still keeps Epiphany as the birthday of Christ; so does the Syrian Orthodox Church in India, though their date is 7 January.

Christmas (i.e. Christ-Festival) was first kept in Rome, on 25 December, the same day as the pagan festival of the Unconquered Sun. The custom was taken up with enthusiasm, and rapidly spread eastwards. Wherever 25 December was accepted, as the date for commemorating Christ's birth, 6 January (Epiphany) ceased to be connected with that event, and was associated with His baptism only. However, when Western Christians adopted Epiphany as a festival they changed its association from Christ's baptism, and instead connected it with His "appearing" to the Gentiles, and especially the "wise men from the east" (Matt. 2.1).

As early as 156 a festival of a different kind was added to the Christian Year, a Saint's Day. On 26 January, 156, the Bishop of Smyrna, Polycarp (p. 24), was burned to death by the Roman authorities for refusing to deny Christ, saying:

"Eighty-six years I have served him . . .
How can I blaspheme my King who saved me?" (Young **350**)

His friends, writing an account of Polycarp's martyrdom, added these words about his grave:

"There we shall gather, with joy and gladness,
to celebrate the birthday of his martyrdom,
to remember those who fought before,
and to prepare those who shall fight hereafter." (Young **163**)

32

This is the first of the Saints' Days, first of an ever-increasing number. A saint is always commemorated on the day of his death, which is his "birthday" into the Church Triumphant.

STUDY SUGGESTIONS

1. It is suggested on p. 19 that three important events which are described in the Gospels all occurred in the same house in Jerusalem.
   (a) What were those events?
   (b) What are the clues in Mark 14.51 and Acts 12.12 which show whose house it may have been?
2. (a) For what reasons were early Christians in the Roman Empire unable to have church buildings in which to meet for worship?
   (b) When and why were the Christians at Edessa first able to have a church building?
3. Read the following passages:
   Acts 16.40; Acts 18.1–4, 7, 18, 19, 24–26; Rom. 16.3–5, 14, 15; 1 Cor. 16.19; Col. 4.15; Phil. 1.2
   (a) Which phrases in Rom. 16.14–15 seem to refer to house-churches?
   (b) Which two verses in these passages refer to house-churches in the homes of women?
   (c) Name the married couple who were connected with house-churches in three different cities, and say which these cities were.
4. The earliest known church building in the world was discovered by archaeologists at Dura-Europos.
   (a) In what year was it discovered? And in what year had the building been altered so as to be more suitable for the holding of services?
   (b) Draw a sketch map to show the place.
   (c) What two things found there would you be likely to find in any church today?
   (d) What ideas about baptism are illustrated by the pictures on the baptistry walls at Dura-Europos?
5. What is the meaning of each of the following words in Greek, and what is each used to mean in the Christian Church today?
   (a) Eucharist   (b) Pentecost   (c) Ichthus   (d) Epiphany
6. (a) In what chief ways were the early Eucharistic services like the Communion service or service of the Lord's Supper in your own Church today?
   (b) In what ways, if any, were they different?
7. What is meant by the statement that "such preaching", i.e. as that of Polycarp, "could never happen again"? (p. 25)
8. Summarize briefly Origen's answers to the following questions about prayer:

(a) How should we pray?
(b) When should we pray?
(c) What should we pray for?
(d) In what position should we pray?
(e) Where should we pray?
In your opinion are these reasons still valid for Christians today?
9. The early Christians held their most important festivals at about the same times of the year as the chief Jewish or pagan festivals.
   (a) Which Christian festivals took place at:
       (i) The Jewish passover?
       (ii) The pagan festival of the sun?
   (b) Why do Christians keep the festival of Easter on a Sunday?
10. (a) Explain in your own words the meaning of the "fish" sign used by the early Christians, and describe some of the ways in which they used it.
    (b) Give an example of any similar religious (or political) sign which people use today, and describe how they use it.
    (c) In what situations do you think a sign of this kind can be most useful?
11. Read Rev. 1.12–15 and 7.9–12.
    (a) In what ways was Perpetua's dream about death (p. 28) like the Day of Judgement as described in these passages?
    (b) In what way was Perpetua's dream like the Eucharist?

CHAPTER 3

The Church and its Mission

In Chapter 2 we saw the first congregation of Christians, who numbered about one hundred and twenty, meeting in a Jerusalem house. It was a small beginning.

About the year 200 Bardaisan, a Christian nobleman of Edessa in northern Mesopotamia (map 4) whom we shall get to know better in Chapter 6, wrote,

"Christ has planted the new race of us Christians in every nation." (Young **14**)

He went on to say that there were Christians as far east as the Kushan Empire, which at that time stretched from Bactria (now Afghanistan) to Kashmir and the Punjab (map 5).

About the same time in the west, Tertullian of Carthage (see p. 23) wrote something strangely similar. People in the Roman Empire, he said, had begun to talk of Christians as "the third race", meaning that there were (1) people of ordinary Graeco-Roman culture, (2) Jews, (3) Christians. He continued:

"But those whom you call *third* race may well become *first*, since there is no nation which has not Christians."(6)

Soon afterwards, about 240, Origen (see pp. 3f) wrote claiming that Old Testament prophecy was being fulfilled by Christianity's becoming a *world* religion:

"By the coming of Christ, the land of Britain accepts belief in the one God. So do the Moors of Africa. So does the whole globe. There are churches now on the frontiers of the world, and all the earth shouts for joy to the God of Israel."(7)

Some of the phrases used, e.g. "every nation", "the whole globe", "all the earth", are obvious exaggerations. But the actual places named are evidence of Christianity's amazing spread, east to the frontiers of India, west to where the African continent touches the Atlantic Ocean, and across Europe to the island of Britain. How had this happened? Who were the missionaries?

THE APOSTLES' COMMISSION:
"TO THE END OF THE EARTH"

For the beginning of the story we turn to the Acts of the Apostles.

There seems little reason to doubt that the author of the Acts was Luke. "In the first book"—which means Luke's Gospel—he had "dealt with all that Jesus began to do and teach" (Acts 1.1). Now he wrote this second book, about all that Jesus continued to do through His Apostles.

As we read the Acts, we may well feel disappointed. The book begins, as Luke's Gospel ends (Luke 24.47), with Jesus telling the Apostles to be His witnesses "to the end of the earth" (Acts 1.8). So we might expect Luke to take the Twelve one by one, and tell us to which country each went, and what all of them achieved. Instead, Luke tells a little about the work of only two Apostles, Peter and John. And he tells us nothing of their going beyond Palestine. No work outside Palestine is mentioned till Acts 11. Then, in Acts 13—28, Luke turns away from the Twelve, to tell of a newcomer, Paul. More than half the book is about Paul's missionary work, through lands north and west of the Mediterranean, till his arrival at Rome. We feel like complaining to the author, "Why is your interest only in Christianity's progress westward? Why does your history lead us to the capital of the Roman Empire, instead of 'to the end of the earth'?"

Before criticizing Luke's work, the Acts of the Apostles, we had better recall who Luke was. In one way he was unique: the only Biblical writer, whether in Old Testament or New, who was not a Jew of Asia. Luke was a Gentile (Col. 4.10–14), and probably a European. There is an early tradition that he belonged to Antioch. He does not mention himself by name in the Acts, but, in 16.10 and other passages, speaks of those who journeyed with Paul as "we" instead of "they". Evidently he joined Paul at Troas and went with him to Philippi. Luke was a medical doctor, and perhaps his home was at Philippi. He may have been the "man from Macedonia" (Acts 16.9) who caused Paul to decide to cross to Europe. Six years later, again at Philippi, he joined Paul's party, travelling to Jerusalem (Acts 20.5—21.18, with "we" all the way). They separated in Jerusalem, but Luke rejoined Paul for the voyage to Rome (Acts 27.1—28.16). The last mention of Luke is in 2 Timothy 4.11, when Paul wrote from prison in Rome, "Luke alone is with me."

So now we understand Luke's interest in Christianity's progress westward—"Come over and help us!" We understand Luke's using half his book to tell of Paul's mission, which he influenced and later came to share. Luke ends the Acts with Paul's arrival in Rome, because the Acts (like the earlier Gospel) was written for Christians in the capital city to read.

In another respect Luke was, if not unique, exceptional. He had learned from the later, mature, thought of Paul his master, that Christ's coming in glory was not to be expected soon. If you believed that the Last Day might be tomorrow, you would not have become a student of history. If Luke had so believed, he would not have begun to write

36

3.1 "Few missionaries had so many advantages as Paul" (p. 7) . . . "Luke ends
the Acts with Paul's arrival in Rome." (p. 36)
An ivory panel of the late 4th or early 5th century shows Paul on his way to Rome,
when he astonished the people of Malta by surviving the bite of a viper after he
had been shipwrecked on the island.

history and thus become the first Church historian. Luke was one of the few who foresaw a long future for the Church here on earth, and a long story of the progress of its mission. So he began to write about that mission's earliest stages, as outlined in the words of Jesus:

"You shall be my witnesses,
1. in Jerusalem,
2.   and in all Judea and Samaria,
3.   and to the end of the earth." (Acts 1.8)

The chart on p. 39 shows what Luke did write.

When we look at the Acts of the Apostles as a whole, as in this summary table, we can see the three stages, not merely as movements from one area to another, but as a widening of the mission's scope.

The author of Acts chose to end his story in Rome. Some scholars have suggested that he may have regarded Rome as "the end of the earth", because peoples from all over the earth could be found there. But that makes Rome the earth's centre, not the earth's end. A better suggestion would be that Luke knew, and his Roman readers might know too, that Paul had hoped to go on from Rome to Spain (Rom. 15.24, 28). Since the American continent was unknown at that time, Spain *was* the earth's western end.

But both these ideas miss the point. In planning his book, Luke thought less of Rome, or Spain, or any other place on earth, than of the scope of the Church's mission. Luke saw that the greatest act of all the Acts of the Apostles was the establishing of the Mission to the Gentiles, which changed the situation for the Church everywhere. Christianity was not to be for Jews and proselytes only; nor was it enough to add Samaritans and Gentile adherents. Christianity was to be the Faith for all men. It would become a *world* religion. That was the meaning of the phrase, "You shall be my witnesses . . . to the end of the earth".

Luke, with his strong western and European connections, did not forget (how could he?) to mention the spread of Christianity from Jerusalem eastwards, further into Asia, and in north Africa. His account of the Day of Pentecost includes a list of fourteen areas from which those who heard the preaching came. Five of these areas were in the east: Parthia, Media, Elam, Mesopotamia, Arabia; and two in Africa: Egypt and Cyrenaica (Acts 2.9, 11). Luke hints that people from these areas were among the three thousand Jews and proselytes baptized and "added that day". He also (as we noticed on p. 16) gives us the first account of a Gentile adherent of Judaism who was baptized a Christian —a man of Africa (Acts 8.26–40). The story is so fresh and vivid, with a style of its own, that Luke may have written it down just as Philip told it, when Paul and Luke were Philip's guests in Caesarea (Acts 21.8). The Greeks did have a system of shorthand.

THREE STAGES	CENTRAL FIGURES: CHIEF EVENTS: PROGRESS OF THE MISSION
1. Witnesses "in Jerusalem" (Acts 1–5)	WITNESS TO JEWS AND PROSELYTES The Twelve, with Peter and John central. Their hearers were men who came from 14 named areas, five in the east, and two in Africa. Three thousand people were converted in one day. Numbers soon rose to five thousand.
2. Witnesses "in all Judea and Samaria" (Acts 6–12)	WITNESS EXTENDS TO SAMARITANS, GENTILE ADHERENTS, AND HEATHEN (a) The Seven, with Stephen and Philip central. Stephen was martyred and leaders scattered throughout Judea and Samaria. Philip preached to Samaritans, and baptized an African adherent of Judaism. (b) Peter in Judea (Lydda and Joppa), and Samaria (Caesarea). Peter baptized a Roman soldier who was an adherent of Judaism and his household. Peter was arrested by Herod, escaped, and fled from Jerusalem. (c) Some of those who had scattered reached Antioch, where Cypriots and Cyrenaicans began to preach to the pagans.
3. Witnesses "to the end of the earth" (Acts 13–28)	THE GENTILE MISSION Prophets and Teachers at Antioch commission Barnabas and Paul, Paul central. Paul's three missionary tours, westward, his arrest in Jerusalem, his defence at Caesarea, and his arrival in Rome.

Chart 2: Three stages in the Apostles' mission

Luke also mentions the part played by men of Africa in starting the Gentile Mission. Some person, or persons, from Cyrene were the first to preach to the pagan inhabitants of Antioch (Acts 11.20). And Cyrene is mentioned again in the account of the prophets and teachers there who were moved by the Holy Spirit to "set apart Barnabas and Saul" (Acts 13.1, 2). Four names are given, two of them being "Symeon called Niger" (which means "the Black") "and Lucius of Cyrene". So men of Africa seem to have had a fifty per cent share in this most important extension of the Church's mission. Luke fails to tell us many things that we might have expected, but we have to thank him for these unexpected items of information.

A few writers in the first and second centuries add a little more about the Apostles, e.g. the martyrdom of Peter and Paul in Rome (p. 68), and John's living to a good old age in Ephesus (p. 24).

Eusebius, the Church historian who collected all the early material which he thought reliable, adds this brief note on two others of the Twelve:

"The Apostles, being spread abroad over the world, Thomas took Parthia, and Andrew Scythia." (8)

We shall deal with this and other traditions about Thomas in Chapter 8. Scythia means the region north of the Black Sea, and Russia regarded Andrew as its patron saint up to the Revolution of 1917. It is strange that we know nothing at all of most of the Twelve.

FULL-TIME MISSIONARIES: "SUCCESSORS TO THE APOSTLES"

For information about the period after the Apostles, we must depend upon Eusebius. He belonged to Caesarea in Palestine. From 231 onwards Origen had brought new fame to this city, and made it a centre of Christian learning (p. 5). Eusebius was there as student, teacher, and writer, and was made Bishop of Caesarea in 313. His most important writing was his *Ecclesiastical History*, in which he gives long quotations from earlier writers. This book is our main source for the history of the Early Church. One section is about "Successors of the Apostles".

Eusebius says that there were too many of these successors for him to name them all, so he mentions only those who still remind us of the Apostles. Some were "shepherds" (i.e. bishops), some "evangelists". He uses this latter word to mean travelling missionaries, as in 2 Tim. 4.5 and Acts 21.8. Among the bishops are Ignatius of Antioch (p. 72), Clement of Rome (p. 24), and Polycarp of Smyrna (p. 24). Even the brief references we make to such men in this book show how they do still remind us of the Apostles.

The missionaries are a more varied company. Eusebius puts first Quadratus, who was famous, with the daughters of Philip (Acts 21.9), for the gift of prophecy. Eusebius did not mean that Quadratus could foresee the future, but that he was able boldly to say, "Thus says the Lord". Quadratus is the earliest of the "Apologists", the name used in the Early Church for those who spoke, or wrote, to defend the Christian Faith. Many of their writings ("Apologies", i.e. "defences") have come down to us, and show us what missionary preaching then was like. For the Apologists tried, not only to win arguments, but to win converts. Quadratus was bold enough to write his Apology as an open letter to the Emperor.

Three missionaries whom Eusebius mentions were philosophers before their conversion to Christianity: Aristides of Athens, Justin who was a student of philosophy at Ephesus (p. 13), and Pantaenus from Sicily (p. 113).

In Chapter 1 of this book, when considering Roman roads and the people who might be travelling, we mentioned "a teacher . . . with ideas which he wanted to make known", (p. 5). In talking of the Greeks, we mentioned philosophy and philosophers (p. 12). It was this profession, the teaching of philosophy, to which these three belonged. Quadratus's "gift of prophecy" sent him to missionary work—preaching. When these wandering philosophers became Christians, they just went on wandering and teaching—i.e. they became missionaries. In doing this, they were indeed successors to the Apostles. They were very like Paul, who went wherever he could get a hearing, and was ready to stay if the opportunity was good. Eusebius says that Justin still looked like an ordinary Greek philosopher, "but he preached the word of God". All three of them wrote Apologies, and Justin was the greatest of them in this. His work was truly missionary, as we have seen on p. 13 and can see again from these questions and answers at his trial in Rome, in 165, when he was condemned and beheaded.

> "Judge: 'Where do you have your meetings?'
> Justin: 'Wherever we can. . . . Our God fills heaven and earth, and is worshipped everywhere.'
> Judge: 'Tell me *where*.'
> Justin: 'I live upstairs in the house of Martin, close to the Timiotinian Bath. . . .
> And if any one wished to come to me there, I passed on to him the true doctrine.'" (Young **47**)

Here we catch sight again of a house-church. Justin could talk to people in the street, and tell those who were interested to come to Martin's house to learn more.

Eusebius says of Pantaenus,

"He was a most learned man, trained as a philosopher. Later he taught at the Christian college at Alexandria. Because he showed such burning enthusiasm, he was appointed herald of the gospel to the nations of the East, and was sent as far as the land of the Indians. He found that people there, who knew of Christ, already had Matthew's Gospel. . . . After much good work, he became head of the college at Alexandria." (Young **34**)

We have already noted the growth of communications from Alexandria eastwards (p. 68). We cannot be sure how far Pantaenus may have gone along this Nile–Red Sea–Arabian Sea route, but Jerome (p. 119), writing about 400, clearly thought that Pantaenus did reach India because he says that this Christian philosopher "preached Christ to the Brahmans and philosophers of India".

Many people today idealize the time when the Christian religion was less organized, more spontaneous. With regard to these early missionaries, to hear God's call and go in faith on one's own may seem a nobler act than to apply to the Church to be accepted as one of its servants and to be sent with the Church's support. But difficulties did arise when a stranger arrived and said he was a visiting missionary.

The Christians in Ephesus to whom the first Epistle of John was written were told:

"Test the spirits, to see whether they are of God, for many false prophets (preachers) have gone out into the world." (1 John 4.1)

Some other very early instructions, not included in the New Testament, were:

"Let every apostle (missionary) who comes to you, be received as if he were the Lord. He shall stay one day, or two, but if he stays three days, he is a false prophet. If he asks for money, he is a false prophet. Not everyone who speaks under inspiration is a prophet; he must also have the manners of the Lord." (9)

And about 170 a pagan writer, Lucian of Samosata, told this story:

"If any impostor comes among the Christians, he can soon grow rich, deceiving these foolish folk. . . . Peregrine left his home country to wander about, and got from them all he needed. They cared for him most generously."(10)

How could a small congregation test its visitor? How could they "receive him, as if he were the Lord", and yet limit his stay to two days? How could Christians be generous without encouraging impostors? Eusebius says that Pantaenus "was appointed . . . was sent", which must mean that he was sent by the Church at Alexandria. As missionary work

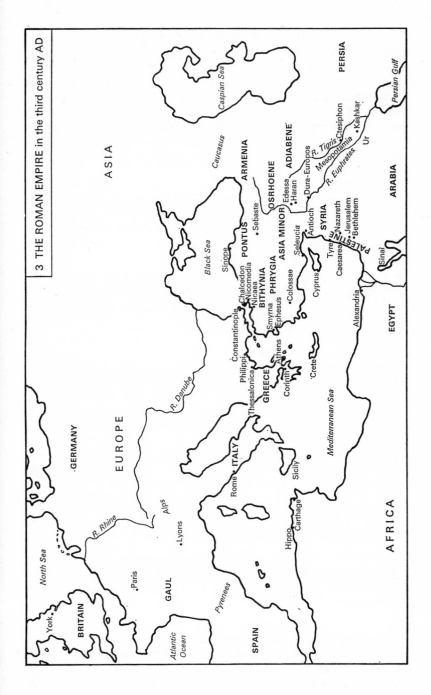

3 THE ROMAN EMPIRE in the third century AD

developed, it had to become the responsibility of the Church, instead of being left to individuals.

Clement was the pupil of Pantaenus, and in 180 succeeded him as head of the college. Alexandria was one of the greatest centres of learning, and Clement continued Pantaenus's missionary work among students. Clement believed that Greek philosophy could be used to provide a reasonable basis for Christian faith, and that the spiritual life is a progress from faith, through knowledge, to seeing God, and, in the life to come, being made like God (p. 60).

And after Clement, came Origen (p. 5). He was less favourable towards the philosophers, but was the greatest of all Christian thinkers. Eusebius says that, although Origen was so young when he began to teach, crowds of students flocked to his rooms to learn how to be Christians, and the city governor posted soldiers round the house to stop them. So Origen kept changing his lodging, now here, now there. Thus the soldiers would be guarding the wrong place, while the students knew where to find him. For a few of his later missionary efforts see p. 132.

Writing in about the year 250, Origen said of general missionary work:

"Christians do all in their power to spread the Faith over the world. Some of them make it their business in life to wander, not only from city to city, but even to villages and hamlets to win converts for the Lord.

If nowadays, owing to the large number of converts, rich men of good position, and women of good family, give hospitality to the missionaries, will anyone dare to say that some become preachers just for the sake of being honoured? To begin with, it was dangerous, and even today there are more non-Christians to despise the preachers than fellow-Christians to honour them." (Young **48**)

Origen went on to answer the taunts of people of other religions who said that Christians accepted even ignorant hearers, by pointing to the popular preaching of pagan philosophers. He said:

"They call men from the street-corners. They do not pick and choose their hearers. Whoever wants to, stands and listens, boys and slaves, and fools. . . . We Christians too want to instruct all men, want to show slaves how to recover freedom of the mind, a mind ennobled by religion." (See Young **52**)

Origen, however, related such evangelistic work to the discipline of the local Church. He says that Christians test their enquirers one by one; then form a class for beginners. Later, there is another class for those who have proved sincere. After a further test, not only of what they

know, but of how they live, these are allowed to prepare for baptism.
One of Origen's former students was one of the most striking missionaries of the third century: Gregory, called *Thaumatourgos*, the "Wonder-worker" (213–270). He was the son of a leading family in Pontus (map 7), south west of the Black Sea, and went abroad to complete his education, hoping to come back to Pontus as a government official. He studied under Origen at Caesarea, became a Christian, came back a missionary, and was made Bishop. His work caused the first mass conversion in the Church's history. This is how it was described by his namesake Gregory of Nyssa, brother of Basil (see p. 151), whose grandmother had grown up among the converts of the "Wonder-worker".

"At daybreak the crowd would again be at the doors, men, women and children, those suffering from demon-possession, or other afflictions, or illnesses of the body. And he would do just what met the need of each who had come. He would preach, he would join an enquiry, he would advise, he would teach, he would heal. This was why so many came to the preaching, because what they saw him do was just as they heard him say, and, through both sight and hearing, he showed them the power of God. For his words astonished their hearing, and his wonders among the sick astonished their sight. The mourner was cheered, the youth was taught self-control, the old got a word of comfort. Slaves were taught to do their duty to their masters; masters were taught to be kind to those under them. He taught the poor that they could be rich in good works; he taught the rich man to think of others, and to remember that he was steward, not owner of his wealth." (Young **58**)

Here we may indeed feel that we have met a successor to the Apostles.
So far we have used the word Evangelist, as Eusebius does, for the full-time missionary. Now we must turn to what today we call Lay Evangelism.

LAY EVANGELISTS

With regard to some of the most important cities, it is impossible to answer the question "Who was the missionary?" We find references to Christians being in a place before any record of missionary work there. For example, in Acts 18 we read of Paul's meeting in Corinth with Aquila and Priscilla, a Jewish Christian couple who had come there from Rome. This is the first reference in the New Testament to Christians in Rome. There is no earlier record of missionary work there. Christianity spread, not only because a few missionaries travelled on the Church's business, but because many Christian laymen travelled on their own business, taking their religion with them.

We see this illustrated if we look again (as on p. 41) at the trial of Justin. Five others were arrested with him. The judge continued the trial with questions to each of these:

"Are you a Christian?"—"Yes, I am a Christian."

"Did Justin make you a Christian?"—"From our parents we received this good confession."

"Who are your parents?"

Different places in Asia Minor are mentioned. The record ends,

"The martyrs went out to the usual place, glorifying God, and were beheaded."

There are two points to notice here:
First, converts to Christianity used to be taught:

"You must be responsible for your sons and daughters, and from their childhood teach them the fear of God." (11)

This is where the passing on of religion begins—in the family.

Second, ordinary people like these, bringing their religion with them and ready to witness to it, were a great missionary influence.

We get one most vivid picture of lay evangelism from the pagan philosopher Celsus, probably of Alexandria, writing about 175. He thought of Christianity as spreading like a disease brought into a great household by the slaves, and then caught by the women and the children. We need not accept as true what he says about Christians teaching rebellion against father and teachers:

"We see in private houses, weavers, cobblers, uneducated country fellows. They would not dare to open their mouths with older people there, or their wiser master. But they go up to the children, or any women who are ignorant, like themselves. Then they pour out wonderful statements: 'You must not take any notice of your father or your teachers. Obey us. They are foolish and stupid. They neither know, nor can do, anything really good. Only we know how men ought to live. If you children do as we say, you will be happy yourselves, and make your home happy also.'

While they are talking, they see one of the school-teachers coming, or even the father himself. So they whisper, 'With him here we cannot explain. But if you like, you can come with the women and your playmates, to the women's quarters, or the cobbler's, or the laundry, so that you may get all that there is.' With words like these, they win them over." (Young 63)

From a Christian writer, probably in Carthage about 200, we get a picture which contrasts with this in one respect—it concerns people who

3.2 "The most convincing way of saying 'I believe in Jesus Christ' is by being ready to die for Him." (p. 49)
Laurence, a deacon at Rome, was martyred in 258, during the persecution of Christians by the Emperor Valerian. According to legend he was roasted to death on a gridiron, as shown in a 5th-century mosaic at Ravenna.

3.3. The martyrdom of Peter and Paul in Rome." (p. 40)
A bronze coin commemorates the two apostles.

were highly educated. Three young lawyers, close friends, spend a day's holiday at the seaside. Two are Christians, the third pagan. Their talk soon turns to religion: Are gods many, or one? Should idols be worshipped? Should we keep to the old ways or judge for ourselves? The account of the long argument ends, "We went home happy, all three. One was happy because he had come to the Christian faith, the others because they had led him to it." The writing does not pretend to be actual history; it is an Apology, by Minucius Felix. But it does represent the sort of thing that happened among the more privileged people.

We learn also of the Governor of a city in Parthia in the year 140. When in the city he kept his Christian faith secret "for fear of the Emperor". But he was so active in spreading Christianity in nearby villages that the pagan priests tried to assassinate him (see p. 94).

In some cases, lay evangelism had the very greatest results. Here are brief summaries of three examples, which we shall study more fully in later chapters.

1. In 264, Goths raided Asia Minor and carried Christian prisoners with them over the Black Sea (map 6). Eighty years later, many Goths were becoming Christians. They had their own bishop and read a Gothic Bible. The Christian prisoners began it all (see pp. 121f).

2. In 294, another Gregory, sometimes called the Illuminator, was consecrated first Bishop of Armenia (map 4). He had been an official under the King of Armenia, but was imprisoned as a Christian. He not only won back the king's favour, but won both king and country for the Christian religion. And he began it all as a layman (see p. 90).

3. In 340 Frumentius became Ethiopia's first bishop (map 5). He and his brother were captured from a Greek ship, when everyone else was massacred. Their Christian witness began as boy prisoners and continued after they became trusted servants of the king (see p. 106).

CHRISTIAN LIVES

The influence of Christian lives is a subject about which most of the Apologists have much to say.

Justin, who knew the roads from Palestine through Asia Minor and the sea-route on to Italy and Rome, wrote,

"Jesus urged us, by patience and meekness, to lead all men from shame and evil desires. And this we can show, in the case of many who have come in touch with us. Many have been overcome, and changed from violence and bullying, by having seen the faithful lives of Christian neighbours, the wonderful patience of Christian fellow-travellers when defrauded, the honesty of Christians with whom they did business." (Young **68**)

Aristides wrote,

"Christians have the commandments of Christ written on their hearts, and keep them, looking for the life of the world to come. . . . They try to do good to their enemies. . . . Their wives are pure, their daughters modest. As for their slaves, they persuade them to become Christians, and then call them brothers without distinction. . . . Falsehood is not found among them, and they love one another. He who has, gives generously to him who has not. . . . And, because they acknowledge the goodness of God to them, lo! there flows forth the beauty that is in the world. . . . Truly great and wonderful is this teaching . . . and there is something divine about it all." (Young **181**)

Boldest of all is the claim of Origen:

"If anyone wants to see men working for the salvation of others, in a spirit like Christ's, let him take note of those who preach the gospel of Jesus in all lands. . . . There are many Christs in the world. . . . Christ is the Head of the Church, so that Christ and the Church form one Body. . . . From the Head to the very hem of the garment, there is something of Christ." (Young **1**)

Some readers may object that the three quotations above are words written by Christians in praise of Christians, and thus are not an independent judgement. But they are words written for critical non-Christians, bidding them to look for themselves, and see.

CONFESSORS AND MARTYRS

Who were the missionaries? We have looked at full-time evangelists, lay evangelists, the influence of Christian lives. Now we must turn to Confessors and Martyrs. From the time of the Early Church onwards, those who suffered for confessing themselves Christians have been called "Confessors", and those who died for doing so, "Martyrs" (from the Greek word for "witnesses"). Behind the use of these two words is the idea that the most convincing way of saying, "I believe in Jesus Christ", is by being ready to die for Him.

Eusebius tells of an army officer in Alexandria named Basilides, about the year 210. Christians heard that he had been imprisoned as a Christian, but there was no Basilides on the Church's list of the baptized. So Christians visited him in prison. He told them that one of his duties had been to lead a young Christian woman to the place of execution. He could do nothing to save her, but had protected her from insults from the crowd. She thanked him and said, "I will ask Christ to reward you". The third night afterwards she appeared to him in a dream, and handed him a martyr's crown. He had decided to be a Christian, even if it cost him his life. They baptized him in the prison, and next day he was beheaded.

Among the last of the martyrs to suffer under the Roman Empire, just before the pro-Christian Emperor Constantine's triumph was complete (p. 78), were forty Christian soldiers at Sebaste in Cappadocia (map 3). They refused to take part in pagan sacrifice, so were marched naked into the ice-cold water of a pool, with a steaming bath on the bank for any who changed his mind. Only one youth, half-dead with cold, crawled out towards its saving warmth. One of the guards saw him, tore off his own clothes, and took his place with the thirty-nine.

Tertullian, as we have seen (p. 23), wrote some memorable words. The best-known are on this subject of martyrs: "The blood of Christians is seed." He goes on to explain,

"The oftener we are mown down by you, the more we increase. Many of your own writers teach men to face pain and death bravely, but they do not win disciples as Christians do, teachers not by words but by deeds." (Young **349**)

He also wrote,

"All who see the endurance of the martyrs, are struck with some doubts, and feel they must look into this matter. Then, when they find the truth, they join up as disciples." (12)

Before Tertullian was converted, he was a lawyer in Rome. So here he may well be describing how he himself joined the side of the Christians.

STUDY SUGGESTIONS

1. (a) Who was each of the following?
   (b) Where did he come from?
   (c) For what reason is he important in the history of the Church?
   Bardaisan   Tertullian   Eusebius   Gregory the "Wonder-Worker"
2. Give examples to show the difference between a "confessor" and a "martyr".
3. What is or was the particular work undertaken by each of the following?
   (a) Evangelist   (b) Apologist   (c) Prophet
4. Into what different countries had Christianity spread by about the year 200?
5. (a) Who called Christians "the third race"?
   (b) Who were "the first race" and "the second race"?
6. "There seems little reason to doubt that the author of the Acts was Luke" (p. 36).

    (a) Was Luke a Jew or a Gentile?

    (b) What was his profession?

7. What command did Jesus give to the Apostles according to Luke 24.44–48 and Acts 1.6–8?

8. (a) Why did Luke devote more than half of his writing in the Acts of the Apostles to details of Paul's missionary work?

    (b) Why did Luke end the Acts with Paul's arrival in Rome?

9. (a) What did Luke see as the greatest act of all the Acts of the Apostles?

    (b) In what way did this act affect the development of the Church?

10. Read Acts 2.1–12.

    Draw a rough map showing the places from which those who heard the preaching on the Day of Pentecost had come.

    Indicate on the map the areas in which each of the following Apostles may have worked:

    (a) Thomas   (b) Andrew

11. (a) Which two of the people named in Acts 13.1, 2 were African?

    (b) What part did they take in the Church's mission?

12. (a) Name four missionaries mentioned by Eusebius.

    (b) What were their writings called?

    (c) What profession did each follow before his conversion to Christianity?

    (d) In what way did each work as a successor to the Apostles?

13. (a) In what way were the early Christians taught to distinguish between the true apostles and false teachers?

    (b) Suggest ways in which we can decide whether a missionary is true or false today.

14. "To hear God's call and go in faith on one's own may seem a nobler act than to apply to the Church to be accepted as one of its servants, and to be sent with the Church's support" (p. 42).

    (a) Do you agree? Give reasons for your answer.

    (b) What opportunities, if any, are there in your own country today for missionaries to work on their own, unsupported by any "sending" Church or organized mission?

    (c) Do you think such unpaid work is more useful than that of an organized mission? What might be its disadvantages and dangers?

15. Why did so many people come to hear Gregory the "Wonder-Worker" preach?

16. "The passing on of religion begins in the family" (p. 46).

    Discuss how you would teach religion to your own children.

17. (a) In what ways is lay evangelism effective today?

    (b) How effective is it in the place where you live?

18. "Celsus . . . thought of Christianity as spreading like a disease . . ." (p. 46).

In what ways have your beliefs been influenced by contact with your family and friends?

19. Many Goths became Christians after raiding Asia Minor and taking home Christian prisoners. The King of Armenia and his people were won for the Christian religion as a result of the imprisonment of Gregory the Illuminator. Frumentius became Bishop of Ethiopia after his capture from a Greek ship by the Ethiopians.

    If you can, give examples from your own experience, or from modern history, of occasions when war or imprisonment helped to spread the Christian faith.

20. Give three examples of ways in which individual Christians today may influence the lives of others.

21. What did Tertullian mean when he said "the blood of Christians is seed"?

CHAPTER 4

Which Scriptures? Which Creed?
Which Ministry?

About the middle of the second century, three groups of people tried to change the direction in which the Church was developing. The first group was dissatisfied about the Scriptures, and said, "Let us, as Christians, stop using the Scriptures of the Jews." The second group was dissatisfied because Christianity was despised by people of other religions for its humble beginnings (e.g. by Celsus, p. 1). They said, "Let us re-state our religion in terms of the highest thought." The third group became excited about inspiration by the Holy Spirit, and about Christ's second coming. These three groups did affect the Church's development, but not in the ways which they had intended. We must look at each of the three groups, naming first one great question, then the man or men who raised the question, and finally the part of the Church's development which they influenced.

WHICH SCRIPTURES?
MARCION, MARCIONITES, AND THE
CANON OF THE NEW TESTAMENT

We saw, in our outline of the Acts of the Apostles (p. 39), that the first Christians were Jews; that the door of the Church gradually opened to admit Samaritans, then Gentile adherents of Judaism, and then converts who had been pagan; and that the crowning event was the beginning of the Gentile Mission with Paul as Apostle to the Gentiles. By the year 150 most Christians were non-Jews. They still read the Jewish Scriptures (the Old Testament, as we call it), but they read them as pointing to Christ, and with Christ as their fulfilment (pp. 13, 14).

In the house-churches some new, Christian, writings had begun to be read. This was not done by any thought-out plan: it just happened. For example, Paul wrote a letter to the congregation at Thessalonica, and put at the end, "This letter is to be read to all the brethren" (1 Thess. 5.27). Later, he suggested that his letters should be passed around from one congregation to another (Col. 4.16). The Jewish Scriptures were read in church, and now Paul's letters continued to be read in church. For this reason people began to call them "Scripture" also (see 2 Pet. 3.16).

As well as letters such as these, the Churches had the words of "eye-witnesses of the Word of life" (p. 25) now written down: what Justin calls "Memoirs of the Apostles" (p. 24), i.e. the Gospels. These, he says, were read as "Scripture" along with the writings of "the Prophets".

Beside all these there were more Christian writings, an ever growing number. Should some of these be counted as Scripture too? If so, which? How many? How should the Churches choose? When should they stop adding to the number? None of these questions had been decided.

At this point, we must turn to the dissatisfied group. Marcion came to Rome about 140. He was a wealthy businessman, and a keen Christian. He owned ships on the Black Sea, which sailed from Sinope, a port midway along its southern shore (map 3). Marcion may have sailed on one of his ships into Smyrna's beautiful sheltered bay and met Polycarp who was bishop there. When later he met Polycarp in Rome, he expected the bishop to know him.

"Marcion asked, 'Do you recognize me?'
'Yes', said Polycarp. 'I recognize you as Satan's eldest son.'" (13)

What had Marcion done to deserve such a rebuke?

In Rome, the Christians had welcomed Marcion. He was a generous man, and gave large subscriptions to the Churches. He was a man with definite ideas, and people crowded round to hear him speak. Marcion loved Paul, the only one of the Apostles (so he said) who had understood the teaching of Jesus. And he spoke very clearly of the difficulties which many Christians felt about the Old Testament. A little later, the anti-Christian Celsus (see p. 1) expressed these difficulties in cruel words:

"Through Moses, God said, 'Kill your enemies, even their wives and little ones.'
Through Jesus, God said, 'Love your enemies.'
Who lied, Moses or Jesus? Or did God change his mind?" (14)

Marcion was preparing to write a book called *Contradictions*, with Jewish Scriptures on one side and Christian Scriptures on the other, to show that they did contradict each other.

But Marcion went further still. As he thought that Paul was the only one to understand Jesus, so Marcion seems to have thought that he himself was the only one to understand Paul. Paul had freed Christians from the Law of Moses (p. 16). Marcion believed that Paul meant Christians to be free from the Jewish Scriptures also, and from the God of the Jewish Scriptures. This God (so Marcion said) rules over the material world, which He created, with all its imperfections; and He acts from no higher motive than justice: "an eye for an eye, and a tooth for a tooth" (Exod. 21.24). This, said Marcion, is not the God of the

4.1. "The Church had to decide which books should be included in the Christian Scriptures . . . distinguishing the true Gospels from the false." (pp. 56, 160) Part of a deacon's duty in the early Church was to guard the sacred books. The mosaic of Laurence's martyrdom shows the four true "apostolic" Gospels: Mark, Luke, Matthew, John, which he had to look after.

4.2 "The words of 'eye-witnesses of the Word of Life' had been written down." (p. 54)
The earliest NT writing that has been found is a fragment of papyrus on which St John's Gospel had been written before the year 156. (Both sides of the fragment are shown in the photograph.)

Christians. The God and Father of Jesus Christ is in heaven; He is pure spirit, and He acts from love.

This answers our question, "What had Marcion done?" We can take the words of Irenaeus, who from childhood had had a close link with Polycarp (p. 24), to express Polycarp's answer. He says:

> "Marcion blasphemed against God . . . put aside much of the teaching of Christ . . . and set himself above the Apostles who handed down the gospel to us." (Young 252)

The Bishop of Rome excommunicated Marcion, and the Churches returned his subscriptions.

Marcion did as many people have done when excommunicated—he took his followers with him. He made Rome his headquarters and used his business connections to spread his sect westward to Gaul, south to the African coast, and east to Mesopotamia.

Having "freed" his followers from the Jewish Scriptures, Marcion announced what, for his sect, the Christian Scriptures were to be. He counted as Scripture ten Epistles of Paul, excluding 1 and 2 Timothy and Titus (perhaps because some people might think that 1 Timothy 6.20 was aimed at him: "Avoid the godless chatter and *contradictions* of what is falsely called knowledge"). He accepted one Gospel only, that of Luke, because of Luke's connection with his beloved Paul. Marcion decided to "correct" even those limited Scriptures wherever (as he said) Jewish influence had altered them. For example, Marcion cut out the beginning of Luke's Gospel, up to 4.31. Marcion did not wish it to be taught that Jesus was a Jew, of Jewish ancestry, born and brought up as a Jew, fulfilling Jewish prophecy. In Marcion's version of Luke, Jesus just appears, teaching in Capernaum. And Marcion altered Luke 16.17, "It is easier for heaven and earth to pass away than for one dot of the Law to become void", to read, "It is easier for heaven and earth, the Law and the Prophets, to pass away, than one dot of the words of the Lord." No wonder that the sharp-tongued Tertullian said, "Marcion teaches the Bible, not with his pen, but with his penknife, cutting out everything which does not agree with his own ideas." Marcionite Churches continued to exist for a hundred and fifty years.

Faced with Marcion's challenge, the Church had to decide exactly which books should be included in the Christian Scriptures. A list still exists which was made in Rome soon after Marcion's time. Of the twenty-seven books of our New Testament, twenty-four are on this list. The reason for choosing them is given. Each has come from an Apostle, though in some cases indirectly, e.g. Mark got the information in his Gospel from Peter (see p. 12), and Luke got much of the information in Acts from Paul (see p. 36). At this time 2 Peter, Hebrews, and James were still in doubt. The list also names some writings which were to be rejected as the work of heretics, adding, "Do not mix *fel* with *mel*." *Fel* is Latin for gall (i.e. bitterness), and *mel* for honey (i.e. sweetness).

The fixing of the New Testament "Canon" (from the Greek word for "rule", or, as here, "list", i.e. of books) began in the west, but its influence spread everywhere. A Chinese inscription at Ch'ang-An, the ancient capital of China, recording Christianity's arrival there in 635, says,

"The Scriptures have been left in twenty-seven books."

West and east, they are the same twenty-seven. Because the fixing of the Canon began so early, Christians were saved from having among their Scriptures late writings of little value, and some writings which were heretical and harmful. So in the end perhaps Marcion did more good than harm to the Church's development.

WHICH CREED?
THE GNOSTICS AND THE RULE OF FAITH

Marcion had tried to separate Christianity from its Jewish origin. Some Christians in the second century went further. They tried to free Christianity from its "small beginnings", which seemed to them unworthy of a great religion: Jesus of Nazareth, Son of Mary, a short ministry in Galilee, death on a cross in Jerusalem. They tried to link Christianity to an impressive set of ideas about the world, and men, and God, which had a great influence at this time. Some of these ideas came from Greek philosophy. Some came from eastern (Hindu, Buddhist, and Zoroastrian) views of life as a conflict between matter and spirit. Some came from astrology and magic. These were the ideas:

The world is made of matter, and matter is evil. The material world is governed from the seven planets by powers which are not good. The world and the planets are ruled by the Creator, a lower god, who made a vast mistake when he came to make men.

Men are composed of body and mind, but in a few men there is a spark of spirit also, shut away in the material body. Spirit should not be in this world at all. That is what is wrong with creation. Here lies the need for a Saviour.

God—the true God, is pure spirit. He dwells, with other spiritual beings which have proceeded from Him, in a realm of spirit and of light, far removed from our dark material world. Because God knew that among men there were a few imprisoned spirits, He let Jesus, who is nearest to God in the spiritual realm, flash upon the earthly scene, to call such spirits to return. Jesus seemed to have a material body and material needs; He seemed to suffer and to die; but this was nothing more than seeming, because Jesus too is pure spirit. Jesus saves by bringing knowledge of the spiritual realm, and of how to return to it. This includes magic passwords which, after death, will carry men's spirits through the planetary powers, past the Creator himself, to the far-off spiritual realm, and to re-union with the true God who is spirit.

Marcion had used his pen-knife to cut out teaching which he did not like. This second dissatisfied group used their pens to add their own kind of teaching. They explained that this teaching was unheard before, because the ordinary teaching in preparation for baptism was enough for most men who had only body and mind. This deeper knowledge had been secretly left by Christ, they said, to be passed on by the Apostles to the spiritual few who could receive it. So they called themselves "Gnostics", i.e. those who have *gnosis*, the Greek word for "knowledge".

Many Christians felt dazzled and dismayed by this teaching. Were these Gnostics really a spiritual aristocracy, they asked. Was simple Christian faith no longer enough?

Let us look at this "simple Christian faith". In the New Testament we find brief confessions of faith, which were used when a man stood before the congregation to be baptized: "Jesus is Lord" (1 Cor. 12.3); "Jesus is Lord, and God raised him from the dead" (Rom. 10.9); "Jesus is the Son of God" (1 John 4.15; adding "Christ" and "Saviour" to this, we get the words whose initials spell "fish", the symbol, which, as we saw, was associated with baptism, p. 23).

When Justin writes the name "Jesus", he often, as if without thinking, adds a phrase about Him: "Jesus Christ, who was born of the Virgin"; "Jesus Christ, who suffered under Pontius Pilate"; "Jesus Christ, who rose from the dead". If you added such phrases together, you would find almost everything that is mentioned in the Creed. Already these facts about Jesus had been set down in the right order, and they were learned and recited by everyone who prepared for baptism.

When Gnostics claimed their deeper knowledge for the spiritual few, Church leaders replied that there was no trace of such fanciful ideas anywhere in the Christian tradition handed down. There was nothing but this one confession of faith, or, as they now came to call it, *Rule of Faith*.

Tertullian of Carthage wrote:

"To find what was the teaching handed down by the Apostles, look to the Churches known to be founded by Apostles. Are you in Greece? Take Corinth or Philippi. Are you in Asia Minor? Then take Ephesus. If you are in Italy, take Rome, where both Peter and Paul poured out their teaching—and their blood. See what Rome has learned and taught, and passed on to Churches in Africa:

One Lord God, creator of the universe,
and Jesus Christ, of the Virgin Mary, Son of God, Creator;
and the resurrection of the flesh.

She unites the Law and the Prophets with writings of Evangelists and Apostles. From these writings she drinks in her faith; she seals this faith with the water of baptism, confirms it with the Holy Spirit; feeds it with the Eucharist, by it exhorts to martyrdom. And she receives no one who opposes." (15)

Irenaeus wrote similarly. His words are especially impressive for two reasons. First, Irenaeus had been taught by Polycarp, who had been taught by the Apostle John (p. 24). Thus he came close to an Apostle. And secondly, when Irenaeus writes of many languages but one faith, we should remember that his Christian life began in Greek-speaking Smyrna, part of his education was in Latin-speaking Rome, as a presbyter of the Church he was sent to Gaul where he preached in a Celtic language, with knowledge of Germans to the north and Spaniards to the south.

"The Church . . . has received from the Apostles and their disciples, this faith:

In one God, the Father almighty,
who made heaven and earth, the seas and all things in them;
and in one Christ Jesus, the son of God,
who became incarnate for our salvation, his birth from
a virgin,
his passion, resurrection from the dead, ascension into
heaven,
and his future manifestation in glory; . . .
and in the Holy Spirit . . .

The Church, although scattered over the whole world, guards this faith as if it lived in one house; believes it as if it had but one mind; preaches, teaches, and hands on these things, as if it had only one mouth; and although the languages of the world are different, the force of the tradition is one and the same. . . .

The Churches which have been planted in Germany, have not believed or handed down anything different, nor have those in Spain, or Gaul, or the East, or Egypt, or Libya, or those in the central regions of the world. The faith is one and the same." (16)

The confession of faith which a Christian made in baptism, had now become the Rule of Faith, to which a Christian must hold fast when others came preaching a different doctrine.

The Gnostics were right, and the Marcionites too, in recognizing that Christianity could no longer be confined within the limits of Jewish thought. Christianity was not to be a sect within the national religion of the Jews; it was to be a religion with a world appeal. The Gnostics' mistake was like that of a man who, in re-shaping his house to give it more room and make it up-to-date, destroyed its foundations. Christianity is a historic religion, founded upon certain events which really happened. The Gnostics ignored many of the facts recorded in the New Testament, and imagined a different Christ, with a different gospel, about a different salvation. For Christianity Gnosticism would have been, not a re-statement, but a ruin. The following words need to be more widely known:

> "The endeavour to give Christ his rightful place in the heart of a people who have not known him—so that he will be neither a foreigner, *nor distorted by pre-Christian patterns of thought*—is a great and exacting spiritual task, in the fulfilling of which a Church can bring a rich contribution of her own to the Church Universal." (17)

One Church leader gave a different answer to the Gnostics, Clement of Alexandria. We have already noticed his attitude towards Greek philosophy, "As the Law educated the Hebrews, so Philosophy educated the Greeks, to bring them to Christ" (see p. 12). Alexandria in this period was more important than Athens itself, as the centre of Greek philosophy. As gateway to Asia it was open to eastern ideas. As Egypt's chief city, it was known as the home of astrology and magic. All this made Alexandria a place where Gnostic teachers flourished. Clement, who wanted to win converts among the educated class, did not believe as the Gnostics did that the material world was evil, nor that salvation was only for the spiritual few. But Clement could, and did, preach the Christian religion as an on-going adventure towards the light. He thought of it as a spiritual progress, beginning here and continuing after death, towards a spiritual heaven and union with God. Here is a sample of his teaching about what true *Gnosis* (knowledge) really means:

> "Knowledge is a perfecting of man, in character, in life, in speech. Faith without searching for God, confesses that God is, and gives him glory. And, starting thus, a man comes to know God, belief being the foundation of knowledge. Knowledge is given by God's grace to those who show themselves worthy. And then, from knowledge of God, comes love, even as it is said, 'To him who has, will more be given' (Mark 4.25). To faith is given knowledge; to knowledge is added love, and to love there comes the heavenly inheritance. This happens whenever a man hangs on the Lord, by faith, knowledge, love, and ascends with him to where God is. . . . This teaches us here the life which we shall afterwards live with God, when, pure in heart, we are at last near to the Lord, and for ever gaze on him. . . . As I have said, the first saving change is from heathenism to faith; the second is

from faith to knowledge; knowledge passes into love, friendship between the one who knows, and the God whom he knows. Perhaps this is what is meant by being 'equal to angels' (Luke 20.36). At any rate, at the end of life in the flesh, we shall continue to advance, through the seven spheres, and into the Father's house (John 14.2), to shine there for ever, for ever without change." (18)

Clement himself says,

"Our teaching may seem to some unscriptural, because so much is not in words of Scripture. Let them know that it is the Scriptures which give our teaching breath and life." (19)

In the teaching of Clement, men of the student class who were seeking something beyond the simple gospel, could see the Christian religion as an impressive structure. Yet they saw it as a structure (this time using the very words of Scripture) "built upon the foundation of the Apostles and Prophets, Christ Jesus himself being the corner-stone" (Eph. 2.20).

WHICH MINISTRY?
MONTANUS, MONTANISTS, AND THE
THREE-FOLD MINISTRY

The third dissatisfied group did not try to turn men from regular Church teaching, but they did begin to follow leaders who were very different from the regular leaders of the Church. They said, "We have returned to the prophets."

The New Testament is full of descriptions of "spirit possession", i.e. of a spirit, generally evil, taking over control of a man. Similar happenings have been known throughout history and all over the world. In some religions, there have been men who were believed to be sometimes "possessed" by a god, i.e. who became the mouthpiece for a god, so that the god could speak to his people.

In the year 156, in Phrygia, the middle part of Asia Minor (map 3), something like this happened to Montanus, a recent convert to Christianity. When he was in a trance, his followers heard him say, in a voice very different from his own,

"Man sleeps, and I awake. Lo, it is the Lord.
No angel, no messenger—I am come myself." (Young 309)

Among the messages was one which said that Christ would soon return and reign from the New Jerusalem (Rev. 21.2), which would be set up at a Phrygian town, Pepuza. Soon Montanus had two women assistants, who went into trances and were similarly "inspired". Some people said that the three of them were devil-possessed. Most thought that this might be an exciting return to the ways of the first Christians upon whom God's Spirit came, and who expected Christ's speedy return. Those who accepted the claims of Montanus said that this was God's final revelation of Himself. They believed that God's Son was about to come in glory, announced by God's Spirit speaking directly to His people. The new messages were written down, to be added to the sayings of the Lord Jesus and the letters of his Apostles. What was the Church to say?

This question has often arisen, and still arises, as movements of emotional excitement appear, whose leaders claim to be inspired by the Holy Spirit, and announce Christ's coming to be near. The movements known as "inspirationism" and "adventism" very often occur together. It is difficult to see how the Church could have said anything but "No" to Montanus's claims. This is the judgement of one leader at that time:

> "It is the false prophet who loses self-control. . . . He begins by wanting to empty his mind, and ends by being out of his mind. They cannot show any prophet of Old or New Testament to have been moved by the Spirit in this way, neither Agabus (Acts 21.10) . . . nor the daughters of Philip (Acts 21.9) . . . nor Quadratus (see p. 41), nor any others at all, except those of their own number." (20)

Division among Christians is always sad, and in some ways the Church's parting with the Montanists was especially sad. Montanists were different from other Christians in some ways but Montanists who died in the persecutions were among the most glorious of the martyrs. The Montanists believed as other Christians did. They lived by Christian standards, with unusual strictness about keeping the fasts, giving to the congregation's needs, no compromise with the pagan world outside, no flight from persecution. At first, Montanists had been forbidden to marry, because of their belief that the end of the world was near; later they were forbidden second marriages. The Pepuza foolishness soon passed, because the Lord had not come. But Adventist movements seem always to survive the disproving of their prophecies. Pepuza became the headquarters of a continuing Montanist Church.

Separation of the Montanists from other Christians was inevitable. Those who did not accept the new prophets seemed to Montanists to "blaspheme against the Holy Spirit" (Luke 12.10). The high moral code of the Montanists, and, above all, their refusal to compromise, won over Tertullian himself in 207. He became leader of the sect in north Africa, where they were often known, not as Montanists, but as Tertullianists. Like many other inspirationist and adventist sects, they found it hard to keep together, but the Montanist Church did survive until the fifth century.

In the Church as a whole, developments with regard to the Ministry were speeded up and extended, not in reply to Montanism alone, but because of all the divisions of this time.

For the early situation we must glance again at the information we have about the beginning of the Gentile Mission. The leaders of the Church in Antioch were "prophets" (inspired preachers) and "teachers". Five are named, including Barnabas and Paul (Acts 13.1). These two, at the end of their first missionary tour, "appointed elders in every Church" (Acts 14.23), i.e. they instituted the local ministry. In doing so, they copied the organization of the synagogue, which was governed by a Ruler and a group or Board of Elders. The Ruler is not mentioned in this passage, but a Board always needs someone to preside. "Elder" is a common word—in most societies a family, a village, or a tribe, is governed by its seniors, i.e. the elders. The Greek word for "elder" is *presbuteros*, which gives us the English word "presbyter" generally used for this officer in the Church.

About the year 58, Paul called the presbyters at Ephesus to meet him, and, addressing them, said, "Take heed to the flock in which the Holy Spirit has made you (guardians)" (Acts 20.17 and 28). Here the Greek word is *episcopos*, which in English was shortened, first to "piscop", then to "bishop". Jerome's comment on Acts 20 is, "The Apostle clearly teaches that 'presbyters' are the same as 'bishops'." The first of these two names ("presbyter") tells us why they were appointed, i.e. because they were more experienced (older), and the second ("bishop") tells what they were to do, i.e. to "guard" the flock. At this stage they may be called "presbyter-bishops". In writing to the Philippians, Paul sent greetings to a congregation "with the bishops and deacons" (Phil. 1.1). The deacon assisted the bishop, as Justin says (see p. 25).

In the year 95, the Church at Corinth was divided and quarrelling, as so often before (1 Cor. 1.11; 3.3; 11.18, etc.). Clement of Rome wrote to try to make peace. He told the Corinthian Christians that the Apostles had founded this two-fold ministry of bishops and deacons, and had provided for it to continue.

> "The Apostles received the gospel for us from Jesus Christ . . . They preached through towns and countrysides, and appointed their first converts as bishops and deacons. . . . And because they knew there would be strife . . . they added a rule that, when these died, other proved men should be appointed. It is not right to expel those who were appointed by the Apostles, or later by other notable men, the whole Church agreeing—men who had done their service without blame." (Young **195**)

The office of bishop grew out of the custom of having a Board of Presbyter-Bishops. We remarked that a Board needs someone to preside. This "president" may, in some places, always have been one particular man, if he was a great man, or if the need for one guiding hand was great. Because of the disagreements during the mid-second century, such need was great everywhere, and the name of bishop came everywhere to mean the one man who presided over the presbyters: *the* bishop in a particular area.

In fixing the New Testament Canon (see p. 57), books were chosen which had come from the Apostles. In defining the Creed, i.e. the Rule of Faith, the standard of belief was the teaching which the Apostles handed down. In the same way, the authority of the Ministry was seen to lie in the fact that it was instituted by the Apostles and was meant to continue in the Apostolic way: i.e. as Clement said, "proved men appointed, the whole Church agreeing".

We began with "prophets and teachers" at Antioch and "presbyter-bishops" at Ephesus. The position from the second century onwards may be illustrated from a letter written to Ephesus by Ignatius, Bishop of Antioch, in the year 107, while he was a prisoner being taken overland by rough soldiers to a martyr's death in Rome. He was more concerned about the threat of divisions in the Churches through whose territory he passed than about his own personal danger. Among the seven of Ignatius's letters which survive, this one, addressed to Christians in Ephesus, is the brightest. One is glad to think that thoughts of music lightened the hardships of his tragic journey (p. 72). Perhaps he knew that in the house-church at Ephesus they sang to the music of the harp.

"You must keep time with the will of your Bishop, as I know you do ... harmonize with the Bishop, as the strings do on a harp. So in your concord and symphony of love, your song is Jesus Christ. Form yourselves into a choir, ... take the key-note of God, that in unison you may sing with one voice through Jesus Christ to the Father." (21)

This shows that in the year 107 Churches in Antioch and Ephesus already had this three-fold ministry. After the far greater dangers of division in the middle of that century, the three-fold ministry would everywhere prevail.

STUDY SUGGESTIONS

1. (a) Which three groups of people tried to change the direction in which the Church was developing in the second century?
   (b) In what particular way did each group try to do this?
2. (a) Give the English meaning of each of the following words:
   fel gnosis presbuteros mel episcopos
   (b) What is meant by the "canon" of Scripture, or of the New Testament?
3. Why did Bishop Polycarp call Marcion "Satan's eldest son"?
4. (a) What was Marcion trying to teach his followers?

STUDY SUGGESTIONS

(b) Which books of the Bible did he recognize as "Scripture", and for what reasons?

5. "Marcion in the end perhaps did more good than harm to the Church's development." (p. 57)
Do you agree? Give reasons for your answer.

6. (a) Summarize in your own words the teaching of the Gnostics about:
(i) the world   (ii) human beings   (iii) God
(b) What reason did the Gnostics give for their claim that this teaching was unheard of before their time?

7. In what ways did the teaching of Marcion differ from that of the Gnostics?

8. How and for what purpose did the Church's "Rule of Faith" come into being?

9. (a) For what reason was Alexandria an important centre for Clement's teaching?
(b) Which famous Christian had he taught?
(c) Explain in your own words Clement's teaching about the meaning of true *gnosis*.

10. (a) What event led people to follow Montanus?
(b) What did Montanus and his followers believe?

11. Give examples to show the meaning of:
(a) spirit possession   (b) inspirationism   (c) adventism

12. (a) What town became the headquarters of the Montanist Church in Asia Minor?
(b) Who became leader of the Montanists in north Africa?
(c) How long did Montanism continue as a sect separate from the rest of the Church?

13. (a) How was the Jewish synagogue governed?
(b) In what ways was the organization of the early Church like that of the synagogue?
(c) Describe the way in which the office of Bishop was developed.
(d) In what ways are the different Churches in your country governed?

14. Ignatius used picture-language about music as used in worship to describe the relationship of a bishop to presbyters and people.
(a) What part does music and singing play in the worship of your Church and of other Churches which you know?
(b) Would the same sort of picture-language be useful in describing the Church's ministry today? If not, what sort would you use?

15. Find out the beliefs of any "independent" Church or sect in your country. Discuss how these differ from traditional Christian teaching, and compare them with the teachings of Marcion, the Gnostics, and Montanus.

CHAPTER 5

The Roman Empire: Through persecution to pro-Christian Emperor

The New Testament reflects the changing situation of the Church in the Roman Empire, from St Paul's time to the end of the first century.

When Paul wrote his Letter to the Romans, about the year 55, he was not only completely loyal to the Empire, but regarded it and its rulers as "agents of God".

> "There is no authority except from God, and those that exist have been instituted by God. . . . Rulers are not a terror to good conduct, but to bad. . . . He who is in authority is God's servant for your good. . . . Therefore one must be subject. . . . Pay all of them their dues, taxes to whom taxes are due, revenue to whom revenue is due, respect to whom respect is due, honour to whom honour is due." (Rom. 13.1–7.)

These last words refer to what Jesus said about paying taxes to Caesar (Mark 12.17). Those who asked Jesus about taxes were trying to trap Him into making either an anti-Roman or an anti-Jewish answer. Jesus used their question as an opportunity to teach that a man's life belongs to God, because he is made in God's image.

Paul, in Romans 13, was concerned with the political situation. His work as a missionary depended on the Roman communications and the Roman peace (see Chapter 1). In this sense, the Roman government was God's agent. Paul hoped that the conduct of Christians in the capital city would show the authorities that although Christians prayed for the coming of a Kingdom which was not Roman, their religion was harmless, non-political, and one which could be left in peace. Christians were at that time being left in peace, and seemed to have a good chance of remaining so.

THE ROMAN STATE AND THE CHRISTIAN CHURCH

The government and people of the Roman Empire were tolerant with regard to religion. The gods worshipped by the Romans were the "powers" upon which they believed that the different parts of life depended: the family ancestors, the guardian gods of house, street, town, trade, crops. The city of Rome was itself regarded as a "power"; in Latin the name was *Roma* (feminine), and so a goddess. The Emperor was regarded as a "power", for the whole Empire depended upon him.

As other lands were taken into the Empire, the Roman officials who had been sent to govern them not only recognized local gods, but were ready to join in worshipping those gods. Here is a description of the situation in the second century:

"Each people has its own national worship and honours its local gods. And the Romans honour them all. That is why their power has filled the whole round world, and spread their Empire beyond the paths of the sun and the bounds of the seas. . . . They reverence the conquered gods, seek out the religions of the foreigners, and make them their own." (22)

One conquered nation, the Jews, refused to allow the Romans any share in their religion. For the sake of peace, the Roman government had to allow the Temple authorities in Jerusalem the right to put to death anyone, even a Roman, who went further into the Temple than the outermost Court of the Gentiles. And when the ruthless Governor, Pontius Pilate, marched his soldiers into Jerusalem, rebellion was about to break out until he withdrew their standards (which contained pagan emblems) from the holy city. The Romans disliked the Jews, and disliked that commandment of theirs which kept them separate: "You shall have no other gods before me" (Exod. 20.3). But they had to allow the Jews to remain separate. We may say that the Roman government was *tolerant* even towards Jewish *intolerance*. As far as religion was concerned, they left the Jews a people apart.

A minority which keeps itself to itself and refuses to share community interests is generally disliked. The second-century Greek writer Celsus makes this excuse for the Jews: "The Jews ought not to be blamed, because everyone ought to live according to the customs of his ancestors." Christians soon began to be suspected.

Christianity had begun within Judaism, and, in St Paul's time, Christians, just like Jews, were being left to go their own way. But it was people like Paul, Apostle to the *Gentiles*, who were making it clear that Christians were not a sect within Judaism. The Church was growing quickly, and the converts were nearly all Gentiles. The Jews often made complaints to the authorities against the Christians. It seemed unlikely that the Roman government would leave Christians in peace much longer. Celsus, whom we have just quoted, continues, "But the Christians have forsaken their national customs for the law of Christ". People do not like a minority, such as the Jews, who shut themselves off from their neighbours. They are still more uneasy when they see a new religion, such as that of the Christians, winning converts at the expense of the old religions. That is a threat to society, as society has been.

THE BEGINNING OF PERSECUTION

Christians were not bad neighbours, nor disloyal subjects, nor plotters against the State. Most of them were ordinary working folk, which in the Roman Empire meant *slaves*. There were (as we saw in Chapter 3) no church buildings, so the Christians met in houses. There was no Sunday rest, so they met at night, when work was done. When people dislike a minority, and think it dangerous, it is easy to imagine dangers which are not there. Someone heard that one nightly meeting of the Christians was called "Love Feast" (Young 152). He passed on the story that, after dinner, they got drunk, and ended with a sexual orgy. At another meeting, words were spoken: "This is my body. This is my blood." And this time the story was that a baby was murdered, to make a cannibal feast. These false stories began quite early. They may lie behind the words in 1 Peter 2.12: "They speak against you as wrong-doers". Probably they are the reason why Tacitus says that Christians in Rome in the year 64 were "hated for their abominations" (see p. 69). We must look at this writing of Tacitus, because it describes an event which caused the first major persecution under the Emperor Nero, in the year AD 64.

On the night of 18 July, night-watchmen in Rome blew their horns, and people awoke to see the city ablaze. Fires were not uncommon, but this one was the worst there had been. Fanned by a strong wind, it burned for six days. A large part of the city was destroyed. Thousands were left homeless. Who was to blame? Rumour said that the Emperor Nero had started the fire. Perhaps, some people thought, he had done so to make way for one of his building schemes. Perhaps, said others, it was just another sample of the wicked ways of a man who had murdered his own mother. The easiest way for Nero to clear himself of this accusation was to fix the guilt upon others, and punish them publicly and severely. The Roman historian Tacitus, who was Governor of the Province of Asia, wrote an account of the fire about fifty years later. In the passage quoted below, four points should be noticed:

1. It is one of the earliest references to Christ by a secular historian.
2. There is an indirect reference to the Resurrection. Tacitus, a non-Christian, does not realize this, but any Christian reader should be able to recognize it.
3. St Peter and St Paul were probably among the Christians who were arrested and killed there, so there is a connection with John 21, where Jesus foretells how Peter would die.

4. Tacitus emphasizes the large numbers of Christians in the capital, only 35 years after the death of Christ.

"Nero fixed the guilt on a class of people, hated for their abominations, who are commonly called Christians (see p. 68). Christ, from whom their name derives, was executed by the Governor, Pontius Pilate, in the reign of Tiberius. . . . Checked for the moment, this deadly superstition broke out again, not only in Judaea, the source of the evil, but even in Rome. . . . An immense number of Christians was arrested." (Young 344)

The executions were turned into a cruel sport to amuse the crowds in the Emperor's gardens. Christians were dressed in animals' skins and hunted by the Emperor's hounds, and the scene was floodlit by other Christians who were burned as human torches. Tacitus adds that Nero himself "mixed with the crowds, dressed like a charioteer, or drove about in a chariot."

Christ foretold that Peter would "follow" Him, and be crucified (see John 13.36; 21.18, 19). Tacitus writes: "Some were nailed to crosses"—among them probably St Peter; many early writers mention his death in Rome. Recent excavations on the Vatican (one of Rome's seven hills), have revealed a monument to St Peter set up there about 160, perhaps to mark his tomb. St Paul, who was in prison in Rome already, was a Roman citizen and so could not be crucified. The early tradition about his martyrdom is that it was "before the rulers" (i.e. in Rome: Clement, 96), that he was beheaded (Tertullian, about 190), and that it was during the rule of Nero (Origen, about 250).

This first persecution did not spread beyond the city of Rome. It was not carried out for religious reasons, but (to quote Tacitus again) was "to satisfy one man's" (i.e. Nero's) "cruelty". The persecution must have made Christians everywhere feel insecure. Men had been put to death just because they were Christians. That might happen again— anywhere and at any time.

We find a description of this kind of insecurity in the Letter to the Hebrews. Scholars have differing ideas about who wrote this Letter, but three things are clear. First, it is connected with Italy (Heb. 13.24). Second, it is written to a congregation, most of whom had previously belonged to the synagogue, but now had committed themselves to a better covenant (Heb. 9.15), a new and living way (Heb. 10.20). And thirdly, it was written at a time when danger threatened. There was no bloodshed yet (Heb. 12.4), but some Christians had lost their property (Heb. 10.34), some had been put in prison (Heb. 13.3), and worse things might follow. "Therefore let us go to him" (Jesus) "outside the camp, bearing abuse for him. For here we have no lasting city, but we seek the city which is to come." (Heb. 13.13, 14.)

5.1–4 Some Roman emperors who persecuted Christians: Nero, Domitian, Decius, Diocletian.

5.5 "Christians were put to death before a crowd in the amphitheatre . . . there were wild beasts to tear and toss them." (p. 73)

Notice the difference between this and the attitude of St. Paul in Romans 13. Rome was no longer the safe, protecting power. Christians had no safety anywhere on earth.

EMPEROR-WORSHIP,
AND THE CONSEQUENCES OF REFUSAL

Still more striking is the contrast between Romans 13 on the one hand, and Revelation 13 where there begins the dreadful picture of a beast with seven heads "and a blasphemous name upon its heads", a beast whom all men worship, except those whose names are in the Lamb's book of life. Still more dreadful is the woman riding on the beast, "drunk with the blood of the saints and the blood of the martyrs of Jesus", and on her forehead the words, "Babylon the great, mother of harlots, and of earth's abominations" (Rev. 17.3, 5, 6).

Parts of the Book of the Revelation are like messages in code. Most of the clues were things generally known among Christians at that time: a few clues are given in Chapter 17. "Babylon", which had been the persecuting power in the Old Testament (especially Daniel 7), stands for the new persecutor, Rome. The "Beast with seven heads" has a double meaning: (a) the City on seven hills (Rev. 17.9), which is Rome; and (b) the seven Emperors from Nero to the then-reigning Domitian (Rev. 17.10). The "Beast" usually means the Emperor, the "Woman" usually means the City (*Roma* in Latin is feminine). "Names of blasphemy" refers to Emperor-worship. Formerly most Emperors had shown little interest in being included among the Empire's gods. They were content just to be revered among the "powers" upon which men's lives depended. But the Emperor Domitian made men call him "Lord and God", the very words which form the climax of the Fourth Gospel (i.e. John 20.28; John 21 is a postscript). It is no wonder that Christians called it blasphemy. The writer of the Revelation turned to the beginning of this same Gospel (John 1.29) and used the words "the Lamb" to mark the contrast and the conflict. And this is what he wrote:

"They will make war on the Lamb, and the Lamb will conquer them, for he is Lord of lords and King of kings, and those with him are called and chosen and faithful" (Rev. 17.14).

We can see why Christians needed a code in order to write of such dangerous matters. An example of Christians who died rather than worship the Emperor's image is described below. It happened in Bithynia in 112. Evidently such a conflict had begun in the Province of Asia in 95, when the Revelation was written.

In 86, under Domitian, the Colosseum was completed—the great stone amphitheatre which remains today the most impressive building in Rome. It used to have marble seats for 50,000 people, and standing room for nearly as many again. And men shouted there, as we do today at a football match. But they were there not to see men kicking a ball, but to watch prisoners (both men and women) made to face wild beasts —bulls, bears, panthers, and lions which were brought to Rome for the purpose. Many Christians were later to die there, the first of whom we know being Ignatius, Bishop of Antioch, in 107.

When an escort of ten soldiers was dragging Ignatius across Asia Minor to Rome, he wrote seven letters which have come down to us, one of which we have already noticed (p. 64). Another of these letters was to Christians in Rome, asking them not to use their influence to try to get him released:

"I know what is best for me . . .
Now I am beginning to be a disciple . . .
Let fire come, or a cross, or facing of beasts, and
    crushing of my whole body . . .
Only let me get to Jesus Christ . . .
Permit me to be a copy of the suffering of my God." (23)

OFFICIAL ROMAN POLICY

We do not know why Ignatius was arrested, but trouble broke out for Christians in Bithynia (map 3) because of their success: the pagan temples were being deserted. In the year 112, Pliny, Governor of Bithynia, wrote to the Emperor Trajan asking how he ought to deal with the growing number of Christians in his province. "There are so many . . . of all ages and both sexes. . . . And it will go on. . . . The contagion spreads. . . . Temples have become almost deserted." Pliny expressed this opinion:

"I find nothing in it (i.e. no sexual orgies or cannibalism), but a base and extravagant superstition."

He had been examining (under torture) "two slave-girls, whom they call Deaconesses". So far, this is what he had done:

"I asked those accused, 'Are you Christians?' If they said 'Yes', I warned them, and asked a second and a third time. If they still said 'Yes', I condemned them to execution. I had no doubt that one must punish obstinacy and unbending perversity. Others I let go, because they recited after me a prayer to the gods, and prayed and offered wine and incense to your image, and, what is more, cursed Christ— things which (so it is said) real Christians cannot be made to do." (Young **346**)

The Emperor's letter in reply said that Pliny was doing right, but that

Christians were not to be sought out. If they were accused and convicted, they must be punished; but anonymous accusations were to be refused, as "a bad example, unworthy of our times".

Tertullian, the lawyer, later attacked the Emperor Trajan's decision:

"Why make Justice play hide-and-seek with herself?
If you condemn, why not seek out?
If you do not seek out, why not declare us innocent?" (24)

The decision, or rather, as Tertullian implied, the *in*decision, was good for the Church, because for most of the time Christian life and witness went on uninterrupted. But Christians lived in uncertainty. Any knock on the door might mean the end of freedom, of peace, of life itself. They were at the mercy of any trouble-maker. Tertullian tells of meetings interrupted by police, of soldiers demanding bribes, of unfriendly neighbours (often Jews), and untrustworthy servants, carrying their tales to the authorities. Evidently their tales were the same old falsehoods about sex offences and child murder.

These same suspicions caused a riot at Lyons in Gaul, in 177. We have an eye-witness account:

"The Christian congregation endured growing attacks from the mob, catcalls, blows, stone-throwing, having to shut themselves in. Then arrest by the officials, trial in the market-place, prison, torture." (25)

Forty-eight Christians were imprisoned there. They were a mixed group; their bishop was ninety years old and there was a boy in his teens. One was a lawyer in the city, another a servant-girl. They were put to death before a crowd in the city's amphitheatre. There were wild beasts to tear and toss them, and an iron chair with a fire under it to finish off any survivors.

Their presbyter Irenaeus was away on the Church's business, so he survived to become Bishop of the scattered flock which remained (p. 24).

CHRISTIANS IN HIGH PLACES

St Paul had said of Christians in his day, "Not many of you were wise . . . not many were powerful, not many were of noble birth" (1 Cor. 1.26). But all the same there were from the start some Christians of influence, e.g. the wife of Herod's steward (Luke 8.3). We may wonder if Christians in that household had a hand in Peter's escape (Acts 12). There were also Herod's courtier Manaen at Antioch (Acts 13.1); members of the Emperor's staff (Phil. 4.21); Sergius Paulus, Proconsul of Cyprus (Acts 13.12).

The Emperor Domitian's niece, Domitilla, wife of a Consul, was exiled in 96, Eusebius says, because she was a Christian. The Emperor Commodus (180–192) was favourably influenced by a Christian concubine, Marcia. The mother of the Emperor Alexander Severus (222–235) sent an escort to bring Origen to Antioch, where (says Eusebius), he "stayed awhile and showed her many things concerning the glory of the Lord". And Origen wrote to the Emperor Philip and his wife (244–249), because he heard of their interest in Christianity. Origen confidently stated that before 248 the old accusations about sexual orgies and cannibalism were "now acknowledged, even by the mass of the people, as false slanders against the Christians". He forecast that:

> "all other worship will die away and that of the Christians alone prevail. It will be so some day, as its doctrine takes possession of minds on an ever greater scale." (26)

PERSECUTION INTENSIFIED

The next Emperor was Decius. In the year 250, for the first time, came persecution which was not local but empire-wide. Decius aimed at nothing less than the destruction of the Christian religion. In spite of his belief in Christianity's ultimate triumph, Origen had seen it coming. He had written in 248:

> "It seems likely that the secure existence, enjoyed by believers now, will come to an end, since those who slander the Word say that there is now so much sedition, because Christians are so many, and because the officials do not war against them as in the old days." (27)

"So much sedition": in the previous forty years the Roman Empire had had twelve soldier-Emperors, six of whom had been murdered. Included in the twelve were a Syrian, an Arab, and a Goth. The year 248 was celebrated as the thousandth anniversary of the founding of the City of Rome, but by then the city was in sad contrast to its former greatness. Why had it declined? "So much sedition: Christians are so many", i.e. people were deserting the pagan gods, and the officials no longer cared. The decline of the Empire was in striking contrast to the advance of the Church. The Church's organization had spread through every province, and to lands beyond. Disputes between Christians were brought to their own bishops, never before non-Christian magistrates. Christian charities helped, not only their own poor, but others besides. If a Christian had to travel to distant places, he carried letters of introduction, and was at once among friends. This was what non-Christians meant when they said that the Christians were "*imperium in Imperio*", a "state within the State". They believed that the State ought not to have any rival. That was why Decius decided to destroy the Church.

We have material handed down through 17 centuries which is as vivid as a newspaper account of happenings yesterday, e.g. (a) a certificate of sacrifice, (b) an eye-witness account of the trial of a Christian, (c) a bishop's statement about how Christians faced the crisis.

(a) A CERTIFICATE OF SACRIFICE

Everyone was instructed to get a certificate, to show that he had obeyed the Emperor's order to worship the gods of the Empire. The certificate was in this form:

"To the Commissioner superintending the sacrifices. I (name), son of (father's name), of (name of place), aged (number of years), identification (marks on face or body). I have always sacrificed to the gods, and now in your presence, according to the order, have sacrificed, offered wine, and eaten of the sacrificial food.

Signed by (name of first witness)
(name of second witness)"
(Young **352**)

(b) A TRIAL

Those who did not get a certificate were arrested, tried, and tortured, to make them obey. Here is a record of one trial, so detailed that the words may have been taken down in shorthand.

"The Proconsul took his seat, and asked:

'What is your name?'—'Pionius.'

'Will you sacrifice?'—'No.'

'What worship do you belong to?'—'I am a presbyter of the Christian Church.'

'A teacher?'—'Yes, I did teach.'

'A teacher of folly?'—'Of religion, sir.'

'Religion! What sort?'—'The religion of God the Father, who made all things . . .' (he is reciting the Creed).

'Well, sacrifice.'—'No.'

'But we all worship gods—heaven, the gods in heaven, Zeus, king of the Gods.'—Pionius was silent, so they strung him up.

Then said the warders, 'Sacrifice!'—'No.'

They tortured him with the iron claw, and said, 'Change your mind. What madness is this?'—'Not madness, it is fear of the living God.'

The Proconsul interrupted: 'Many have sacrificed, and are alive and in their right mind.'—'I cannot.'

'But now that you have been cross-questioned, think about it to yourself a moment, and change your mind.'—'Not I, sir.'

75

One of the bystanders called out, 'Why are you so determined upon death?'—'Not upon death, upon life.'" (28)

(c) HOW CHRISTIANS FACED THE CRISIS

It had been safe to be a Christian for so long that no one thought of danger. Suddenly Christians saw before them prison, torture, death. Cyprian, Bishop of Carthage, wrote:

"Many were conquered before the battle, ran to the market-place of their own accord, as if they had always desired the chance to sacrifice. Why, wretched man, do you bring an animal to offer? You have come to sacrifice yourself, to burn up your Christian faith in the altar's fire." (29)

Cyprian quotes with sympathy this confession:

"My mind stood firm. My faith was strong, my soul struggled long, unshaken by the torturing pains.
   But when, wearied out as I was, the whip was now tearing me, the clubs bruised me, the rack stretched me, the iron claw dug into me, the fire roasted me—my flesh failed me in the fight, the weakness of my body gave way." (30)

Cyprian praises those who suffered, martyrs and confessors.

"The white-robed regiment of Christ's soldiers is here,
who, in standing fast, have broken the attack.
To the world you have fought back bravely,
to God you have offered a glorious triumph.
You have been a pattern to your brothers who shall follow you." (31)

In 250 Cyprian went into hiding, in order to stay alive and lead his people. Under Decius's successor, Valerian, he let himself be arrested, and when his judge said, "You shall be executed with the sword," Cyprian simply replied, "Thanks be to God."

Valerian's policy was to execute bishops and senior clergy, and thus leave the Church leaderless. But the Empire was disturbed by both barbarian and Persian invaders, and Valerian's plans were not fully carried out (see p. 97). The next Emperor, Gallienus (261), stopped persecution as unlawful, gave back Church property, and granted toleration to Christians. Everyone thought that the longed-for peace had come.

THE FINAL PERSECUTION

In the year 284 came the Emperor Diocletian, who instituted the "Tetrarchy"—the Empire ruled by Four. Diocletian was a soldier who

5.6 "Christians were in some of the highest places in the state." (p. 78)
And some Christians were very wealthy. This richly ornamented silver casket carries the portraits of a well-to-do couple. The Latin inscription on it shows that they were Christians.

had risen from the ranks to become Captain of the Imperial Body-guard, and in 284 Emperor. In 293 he set up a new order of government for the Empire. There were two Emperors: Diocletian, Emperor in the East, with Galerius as his assistant, and Maximian, Emperor in the West, with Constantius as his assistant. The two assistants were given the title "Caesar". In 305 the two Emperors would retire, and the two Caesars become Emperors, with new Caesars appointed. The two Emperors were meant to join in defending the long Rhine–Danube frontier against barbarian invasion, and the two Caesars to secure an orderly succession of rulers.

Since toleration was granted in 261, the Christian religion had been favoured. Christians were in some of the highest positions in the State. In most cities and towns in the east they had built great churches. The Emperor Diocletian's wife and daughter were known to be pro-Christian.

Then suddenly in 303 Diocletian ordered that churches should be pulled down, Bibles and other Christian books should be handed over to be burned, and all Christian worship should cease. Soon clergy were arrested. In 304 all citizens were commanded to sacrifice to the Roman gods or die. Why did Diocletian suddenly order this change?

In Diocletian's new government, there was a great contrast between the two Caesars. Galerius in the east was bitterly anti-Christian. It was he who persuaded Diocletian that Christians were a danger. Constantius in the west (says Eusebius) "worshipped one God alone", whom he vaguely connected with the sun. But Constantius's family must have been influenced by Christians; one of his daughters had been given a Christian name, Anastasia (meaning "Resurrection"). In the west, under Constantius' rule, there were no martyrs. Throughout the Eastern Empire the blood of many Christians was shed.

Eusebius wrote of the sufferings of this time, both in his *Ecclesiastical History* and in a small book, *The Martyrs of Palestine*, and he wrote much of it as an eye-witness. How he managed to travel about, and to keep free (except for one short time in prison), we do not know. Probably he had powerful friends.

Eusebius saw churches pulled down, Scriptures burned in the market-place, and bishops and presbyters hunted, jeered at when caught, and crowded into prisons to wait their turn to die. He tells of terrible mass murders. In Phrygia, a church was surrounded and set on fire with its congregation, the whole village, inside it. In Nicomedia (map 3) people were bundled into barges, taken out to sea, and thrown overboard. In Egypt, there were beheadings "till the executioners grew weary". When deaths became too many, the penalty was sometimes changed to forced labour in the mines, gouging out one eye from each man or woman, and burning the tendons of one leg, so as to make their escape impossible.

PERSECUTION ENDED—
THE FIRST PRO-CHRISTIAN EMPEROR

Three dramatic events point to the end of this last and fiercest persecution:
1. The flight of Constantius' son, Constantine, from Galerius' court, in 306.
2. The toleration edict of Galerius, in 311.
3. The battle for Rome, in 312.

THE FLIGHT OF CONSTANTINE, 306

As Western Caesar, Constantius went off to Gaul (now France), leaving his son Constantine in Diocletian's care. In 305, the Eastern Caesar, Galerius, took Diocletian's place as Eastern Emperor. This was an unwelcome change. To Constantine, Galerius seemed more like a jailer than a guardian. In 306 Constantine decided to escape and go to his father, who had been the Western Emperor since 305. Constantine rode swiftly across Europe, by using the stables where imperial messengers could change horses every few miles. At each stage he secretly lamed every horse except the one which he took, so that no one could pursue him. He joined his father in Gaul, crossed with him to Britain, and was with him when he died in York. The army hailed Constantine as their Emperor.

THE TOLERATION EDICT OF GALERIUS, 311

In 311 Galerius, Eastern Emperor and arch-persecutor of Christians, was dying. He was afraid of death and of hell, which is not surprising. His edict acknowledges defeat.

> "Because great numbers of Christians still persist, we with our usual mercy, have thought it right to permit them again to be Christians, and to hold their religious meetings. So it will be the duty of Christians, because of this toleration, to pray to God for us, for the State, and for themselves." (Young **359**)

So passed the last of the persecutors from the throne of the Empire. The Christians had triumphed.

THE BATTLE FOR ROME, 312

Constantine was not the only "Emperor" with an army in the field. In 312 he faced his last rival at the Milvian Bridge over the river Tiber, outside the walls of Rome. After the next day's battle, either he or his rival would rule in the western capital. The other would be dead. Eusebius wrote about that evening:

79

5.7 and 5.8   The emperor Constantine went into battle under this Christian sign—and won (p. 80)

A huge statue of him, put up in 320 and now in the Church of St John Lateran in Rome, is among the many memorials of his triumph.

"Constantine now turned to his father's God in prayer, imploring God to tell him Who He was, and to help him in his present troubles. It would be hard to believe, if the Emperor himself had not told me, when I had the honour to know him, and he swore that this was true. He saw a cross of light in the sky, and the words, 'In this sign conquer'. Night came, and in his sleep he dreamed that Christ came with the same sign, for him to copy, as a guard against his enemies. I have myself seen the copy which the goldsmiths made for the Emperor next morning—a lance covered with gold, turned into a cross with a bar going over it; and on the end of the lance a garland of gold and gems; and inside this the two letters X (i.e. Ch) and P (i.e. R) which stand for the Saviour's name, the letter X cutting across the centre of the letter P." (32)

This means the first two Greek letters for "Christ" were run together in the monogram ✴ . This was often later simplified to ✗ , and often the cross was stood upright ⚧ . From this time on the sign of the cross was used by Christians everywhere. It has always stood, not only for the cross on which Christ died, but for Christ Himself.

Constantine went into battle under this Christian sign. The inscription on the Arch of Constantine, which still commemorates his victory in Rome, says the victory was "at the instigation of the Deity".

If Constantine said he saw a cross and heard a message about victory, Eusebius (who saw with his own eyes the worst of the persecutions, and was close to this first pro-Christian Emperor soon after his victory) had a vision of what lay ahead:

"How wonderful is the power of Christ, who called obscure and ill-educated men from their fishermen's trade and made them the law-givers and teachers of mankind! 'I will make you fishers of men,' Christ said, and how well he has fulfilled the promise! He gave power to the Apostles, so that what they wrote should be translated into every language, civilized and barbarous; should be read and pondered by all nations; and the teaching should be received as the revelation of God. . . . Victorious over gods and heroes, Christ is making himself alone, in every region of the world, acknowledged by all people as the only Son of God." (33)

The change was vast—from persecution to Imperial favour. One incident will illustrate it. Not many years before, the Emperor Diocletian had ordered Bibles to be burned, and Eusebius had watched them burning in the market-place. Now, as bishop in his beloved Caesarea (with its library and its copyists of manuscripts restored), Eusebius had the pleasure of receiving this letter from the Emperor Constantine about the new—and Christian—capital city which he had founded, Constantinople:

"Many people are joining the Church in the city which is called by my name. The number of churches must be increased. I ask you to order fifty copies of the Holy Scriptures, to be written legibly on parchment, by skilful copyists . . . as quickly as may be. You have authority to use two government carriages to bring the books for me to see. Send one of your deacons with them, and I will pay for them generously. God keep you, dear Brother!" (34)

The change was so vast that Eusebius wrote as excitedly as if the Kingdom of God had come on earth. The Church was now to be faced with dangers that were different from persecution—the danger of worldliness, misuse of power, lowering of moral standards. But Eusebius was right. Christians in this western part of the world had the opportunity, which no Christians had had before them, to influence a whole civilization and to turn it in a Christian direction.

STUDY SUGGESTIONS

1. Read Romans 13.1–7.
   (a) For what particular reason was Paul anxious that the Roman authorities should regard the Christian religion with tolerance?
   (b) Compare Paul's attitude towards the state as shown in Rom. 13.1–7 with that of Jesus in Mark 12.17 and that of the writer in Heb. 13.13, 14.
   (c) Do you think that political "rulers" today are "instituted by God"? Are they always a "terror" to bad conduct?
   (d) To what extent do you think Christians today ought to follow Paul's teaching in this passage?
   Give reasons for your answers to (c) and (d).
2. (a) What was the attitude of the Romans to the religions of the lands they had conquered?
   (b) What was the Jewish attitude to the Romans?
3. Read Deut. 23.15, 16 and 24.14, 15; Eph. 6.5–9; and Col. 3.22—4.1.
   (a) What was the Jewish law about the relationship between slaves and their masters?
   (b) What was Paul's teaching on the subject?
   (c) Compare both with present-day relations between workers of different kinds and their employers in your country. Do you think such matters should be regulated by law? Give reasons for your answer.
4. (a) Who was the "Apostle to the Gentiles"?
   (b) Where is the Colosseum?
   (c) What is the "City on Seven Hills"?
   (d) Who were the following?
      Cyprian Ignatius Domitilla

(e) Explain what is meant by *imperium in Imperio*.

(f) What did the Emperor Decius plan to do in the year 250?

5. (a) Describe the event which led to the first major persecution of Christians in Rome, and the scene at the executions.

(b) Discuss any other examples of which you know, where a group of people has been made a "scapegoat", i.e. been blamed for a disaster for which they were not responsible.

6. For what chief reasons did the Roman authorities regard the spread of Christianity as a threat to the safety of the Empire?

7. Why are parts of the Book of Revelation written like messages in code? Give examples of this code.

8. Which Roman Emperor in 261 stopped persecution as unlawful?

9. (a) What was the "tetrarchy"?

(b) Who instituted it? and when?

(c) Give the titles and names of the first rulers in the tetrarchy.

10. (a) Explain why in 303 Diocletian suddenly ordered all Christian worship in the Empire to stop.

(b) Describe the three events which led to the end of this last persecution by Diocletian.

11. (a) Who was Pliny?

(b) To whom did he write concerning the growing number of Christians?

(c) How was he told to deal with them?

12. (a) Who was the first pro-Christian Emperor?

(b) What was the name of the capital he founded?

13. (a) For what does the sign of the Cross stand?

(b) In what ways was it used by the early Christians?

14. (a) Give examples of Christian people in your country who have suffered for their faith.

(b) In what ways do you think that faith can be strengthened by persecution?

(c) Discuss the ways in which Christians can be helped to face and bear persecution.

15. (a) What other dangers does the Church face, besides persecution?

(b) How can Christians combat these dangers?

CHAPTER 6

First Christian Kingdom and First Christian Nation

THE KINGDOM: EDESSA

We have already noticed the hint in the Acts of the Apostles that from the very beginning there may have been converts from among the "Parthians, Medes, Elamites, inhabitants of Mesopotamia" who were in Jerusalem on the Day of Pentecost (p. 38), that is to say, from countries further east. We must now look for more definite evidence of Christianity's progress in this eastward direction.

The first stage in that progress was a short one, from Antioch—where, as we have seen (p. 36), St Paul's westward mission began—eastward a hundred and thirty miles, to Edessa (map 4). It was a short step, but one which led to a different part of the world. Antioch belonged to the Mediterranean area. It ranked as third city of the Roman Empire —after Rome and Alexandria. Edessa was the capital city of the small independent kingdom called Osrhoene, looking mostly east and south. This city was near a caravan route which had been used since before Abraham's time. Haran (Gen. 11.31) lay a few miles away. Edessa was also on a tributary of the great river Euphrates, flowing south to the Persian Gulf—so it was in a strategic position for further advance eastwards. And the ruler of this little kingdom became the first Christian king. No wonder that there were romantic stories about this!

When Eusebius was writing his *Church History*, about the year 320, he visited Edessa, and found records of letters which were said to have passed between Abgar, King of Edessa, and Jesus Himself. The letter which was supposed to be Abgar's said:

> "I have heard of you, that you heal without medicines or herbs, making the blind see, the lame walk, the leper clean. . . . I beg you to come and heal me. I have heard that the Jews wish to harm you. I have a city, very small, but stately. It would do for us both." (35)

And here is the supposed reply:

> "Blessed are you that have not seen me but have believed. I must finish here all that which I was sent to do, and then return to Him that sent me. But after that, I will send one of my disciples to heal you, and to bring life to you and those with you." (36)

The record went on to say that, after the Ascension, the Apostle Thomas "sent Thaddeus (or in Syriac, Addai), one of the seventy" (Luke 10.1), to Edessa. Thaddeus healed Abgar and "many others in the city, did marvellous works, and preached the word of God."

Can this be true? Eusebius believed so, but other evidence suggests that he was mistaken. The coin shown on p. 88 bears the head of King Abgar, with a cross on his head-dress showing that he was a Christian. However, this is not the Abgar who lived at the time of Jesus, but Abgar VIII, and the coin—which is now in the British Museum collection —was issued in the period 180–192. The compilers of the records of Edessa have taken a real event, the conversion of their king, and tried to make it more glorious by pretending that it happened at the time of Jesus Himself. But to be the first Christian king, first to acknowledge Christ as King of kings, is glory enough.

Besides having the first Christian king, Edessa may have had two more "firsts"—the first church building, and the first translation of the Greek New Testament into another language. The history of Edessa tells of a flood in the year 201:

> "Abgar the King stood on the tower, called the Persian tower, and watched the waters by the light of torches. The waters broke against the western wall of the city, entered the city, and overthrew the great and beautiful palace of the King. . . . And the waters destroyed the temple of the church of the Christians." (Young 9)

There were no church buildings in the Roman Empire at this time (p. 20). But this record shows that in Edessa the Christians were favoured by the king, and had a church close to the palace.

Edessa became the home of Syriac literature. Syriac was then the spoken language of most parts of Mesopotamia. It was closely related to Aramaic, the spoken language of Palestine. From the second century onwards Christians translated Greek writings into Syriac, and wrote some original Syriac works. The Syriac New Testament may be the earliest of translations made from the Greek, well before 200.

The Syriac language, as developed in Edessa, is important because it became the ecclesiastical language of the eastward-advancing part of the Church, and was carried, in Scriptures and Liturgy, right across Asia to the China Sea.

TATIAN AND BARDAISAN

The outstanding figures among early Christians in Edessa were Tatian and Bardaisan. Tatian was born in Mesopotamia. He grew up speaking Syriac, and received a good education, and then wandered westward, seeking a religion which would satisfy him. He tried many religions before his search ended, soon after 150, among Christians in Rome. This is how he describes the appeal of the Bible, in contrast to the pretended mysteries of other religious books:

> "I put my trust in these Scriptures, because the style was not fanciful, the speakers were genuine, the composition was easy to understand, future events were foretold," (he means prophecies about Christ's coming) "messages were far more than one could have expected, and the universe had one guiding principle.
>
> Taught by God, I came to understand that here was a religion which sets us free from the bondage that is in the world, snatches us from rulers many, yes, from ten thousand tyrants." (Young **78**)

The above quotation is from Tatian's one surviving writing, *An Address to the Greeks*. It shows how strongly he reacted against all that belonged to Greco-Roman civilization. His one positive note is thankfulness for being delivered from the innumerable gods and spirits of polytheism.

Justin had been Tatian's teacher in Rome, and after Justin's martyrdom in 165, Tatian himself took up Justin's work as a teacher. Clearly it must have been teaching of a narrower and more negative kind.

Tatian's most important contribution may have been made after his return to Mesopotamia, about 172. He wrote, either in Syriac or in Greek, what has been called the first Life of Christ. Its actual title is *Dia-tessaron*, which is Greek for "From Four", i.e. one Gospel made from four. Until the fifth century, Syriac-reading Christians used this book more than they used the four Gospels themselves.

Bardaisan was born of a noble family in Edessa in 154. He was attached to the court, and became a Christian in 179, at about the same time as King Abgar. He was a man of independent thought, a poet, and he became the first writer of Syriac hymns. One of his pupils recorded Bardaisan's teaching in a book, *Concerning Fate*. It is written in the form of questions from an enquirer, and Bardaisan's answers. They began by discussing the problem of evil. Bardaisan says that if man had been made without freedom of choice, he would have become a machine. Yet man is not entirely free. He does not choose his place or the conditions of his life. Some things are fixed by nature, and some by what Bardaisan calls "fate". Nature, fate, and freedom together make the pattern of a man's life. But God gave man sufficient of this third element, freedom, to make him able to choose *how* he will live. Bardaisan illustrates this by pointing to:

> "the new race of us Christians, which Christ has planted in every nation. Wherever we are, we are called by the one name, Christian. . . . Our brothers give up national customs which are contrary to their Christian faith". (Young **14**)

He shows how the one Christian moral standard is observed by Christians, whatever different "nations" they belong to, mentioning Parthians, Gilanians, Kushans, Persians, Medians, and people of Edessa. Map 4 shows that about the year 200 Bardaisan knew of Christians over a wide area of Asia, up to, or approaching, the borders of India (p. 101).

The most beautiful Christian Syriac poem is *The Hymn of the Soul*, which was written, if not by Bardaisan himself, by someone belonging to his circle. The words are written as from one who, born the son of a king, was sent on a long journey to fetch from Egypt a pearl, which was guarded by a serpent. Alone in a foreign land, he dressed like the people there, ate their food, and forgot the land of his birth and the pearl which he had been sent to find. His parents were grieved and wrote an urgent letter. The letter flew through the sky, landed beside him, and spoke to him in the language of his own country.

"So I remembered my royal birth and my free born nature,
Remembered the pearl, for which they had sent me to Egypt,
and I began to charm the terrible loud-hissing serpent.
Down he sank into sleep at the sound of the name of my Father,
And at my Brother's name, and the name of my Mother the Queen.
I seized the pearl, and homewards started the journey."
(For the whole poem, see Young 13)

Some call this poem "The Hymn of the Redeemer", and think that it is about Christ's Incarnation. But Christ did not forget His divine nature, nor His Father's will for Him. It seems more likely that the subject of the poem is the human soul, which is made to belong to God, but which forgets Him, is re-called by the Gospel, and is baptized in the name of Father, Son, and Spirit. The word for "Spirit" is feminine in Syriac, and so the Spirit is sometimes called "Mother". The poem ends,

"I had performed His command, and He had fulfilled what
He promised,
With favour received me, and near Him I dwell in His
Kingdom."

It is good to read this poem, and to think, not of the Gnostics' fanciful ideas of salvation as some have done, but of the simple words of Jesus about the Kingdom of heaven, a pearl of great value, and a man giving all he has to get it (Matt. 13.45, 46).

This poem, although originally separate, has come down to us as part of the document called *Acts of Thomas*. This document *is* Gnostic, and fanciful, but it contains references to India which might have some historical value, and which we shall consider in Chapter 8.

Tatian began as a disciple of Justin, and Bardaisan was highly praised by Eusebius, but both these great figures of the "Syrian"

6.1 Abgar VIII of Edessa: "first
Christian king". (p. 85)
Coins issued during Abgar's reign show
a cross on his headdress.

6.2 The Persians under the Sassanid dynasty took over the Parthian Empire
(p. 89). They proclaimed their king Ardashir as first emperor. (p. 95)
A rock-carving at Naqsh-i-Rustam in Iran shows Ardashir (on the left) receiving
a diadem, symbol of kingship, from the Parthians' god Ormazd.

Church were, and still are, counted as heretics by most Western Churches. They deserve more kindly treatment, as Christian thinkers making the first attempts at a non-Greek expression of Christian truth.

THE NATION: ARMENIA

Another country to the east of the Roman Empire, but further north, was Armenia (map 4). This too, like Edessa, was a scene of early Christian success. Eusebius lived and wrote at the very time of Armenia's becoming Christian, and he mentions it in his *Church History*, but without giving details. Writing of the final persecutions in the Roman Empire, he says that the Romans in 311:

> "Went to war with the Armenians, who from old times have been friends and allies of the Romans. The Armenians were now also Christians, zealous in their piety towards God, so the enemy of God (the Emperor) tried to make them sacrifice to idols." (37)

The Greek historian Sozomen, in his *Church History* written about 450, has more to say:

> "Tirdat, King of Armenia, became a Christian, because of a sign from God in his own family, and proclaimed to all his people that this should be their religion. The Armenians, I have understood, were the first to accept as a nation the Christian faith." (Young 37)

Here is the evidence that Armenia was the first Christian nation, but no Greek writer seems to have recorded the whole story. So we turn to an Armenian, Agathangelos. He wrote as though he was living at the time of his country's conversion, but probably his date was about 450.

The small nation of Armenia lay between the empires of Parthia to the east, and Rome to the west. Armenia's policy was to seek the protection of one of these empires whenever she felt herself threatened by the other. In the year 224 the Persians, under the Sassanid Dynasty, took over the Empire of the Parthians. Their strength seemed so threatening that King Khosrov of Armenia tried to make an alliance with Rome. The Persians answered by getting an Armenian noble, Anak, who was related to Khosrov, to assassinate him. Anak was executed for the crime with all his household except for one child, who was carried off to Roman territory. This child was brought up as a Christian in Cappadocia (where Christians were many), and was given the name of Gregory. The invading Persians then seized Khosrov's family, but again one son, Tirdat, escaped, and grew up to be a soldier of distinction in the army of the anti-Christian Roman Emperor, Diocletian. In 286, with Diocletian's help, Tirdat regained his father's throne. Gregory returned too, and became one of Tirdat's most trusted officials in the re-making of his kingdom. But Gregory, as a Christian, refused to join in the king's worship of Armenia's guardian goddess. The king had him imprisoned and tortured. Then, discovering that Gregory was the son of Khosrov's murderer, Tirdat condemned him to a dreadful death. But a Christian woman servant in the palace secretly saved Gregory, and many misfortunes came upon King Tirdat, till at last his sister dreamed that "Gregory alone has the medicine for all the country's ills", i.e. that Gregory's Christian religion would save Armenia.

It is not strange that religion should have contributed to Armenia's independence. The Sassanid kings had made Zoroastrianism Persia's national religion. This religion, which is called after its founder Zoroaster, still survives in India under the name of Parseeism, which means "Persian-ism". Zoroastrians believe in one God, and hold a high moral standard. The Armenians at that time did not want to adopt anything Persian, but some were asking where else they might find for themselves a more worthy religion. Christianity was rapidly becoming the majority religion in parts of the Roman Empire, though there was still the final persecution (303–311) to be faced. Nowhere was Christianity stronger than in the province of Cappadocia from which Gregory had come. So the Armenians listened to Gregory's teaching, and the king decided for the Christian religion. Throughout Armenia idols were destroyed, temples were cleansed and consecrated as churches, and many of their priests became Christian clergy. Until this time Gregory was a layman. The Bishop of Caesarea in Cappadocia consecrated him as Armenia's first bishop in the year 294. A later bishop developed a new alphabet for the Armenian language, and the New Testament appeared in that language by the year 410.

Armenia truly was "the first to accept as a nation the Christian faith".

STUDY SUGGESTIONS

1. Draw a rough map showing Osrhoene and Armenia, and mark the city of Edessa.
2. (a) Who was the first Christian king?
   (b) Where was the first known church building and how was it destroyed?
3. (a) Which important language was probably the first into which the New Testament was translated from the Greek?
   (b) Where was this language spoken?
4. (a) Where was Tatian born?
   (b) Who was his teacher in Rome?
   (c) What was Tatian's most important writing?
   (d) What was his opinion of the Greco-Roman civilization?

5. (a) Who was the first writer of Syriac hymns?
   (b) What was his answer to the problem of evil? Do you agree?
   Give reasons for your answer.
6. (a) Tell in your own words the story of the "Hymn of the Soul".
   (b) Compare this story with the story in Matt. 13.45.
   (c) Give examples of Christian poetry in your own language.
7. (a) Name three writers to whom we owe our knowledge of the
   history of the Church in Armenia.
   (b) Under which king did Armenia become the first Christian
   nation?
   (c) Describe in your own words, starting from the assassination of
   King Khosrov, the events which led to King Tirdat's becoming a
   Christian.
8. (a) What was Persia's national religion at the time of the Sassanids?
   (b) Where does it survive in the world today and under what name?
   (c) What do its followers believe?
9. (a) Who became Armenia's first bishop, and when?
   (b) When was the New Testament first translated into Armenian?
10. (a) In what way did religion contribute to Armenia's independence?
    (b) What effect, if any, does religion have on the national life of
    your country today?

CHAPTER 7

Parthia/Persia: through persecution to toleration

THE EARLY CHURCH IN PARTHIA

Eastward of the city-state of Edessa, and of the small nation of Armenia, lay the Parthian Empire (map 4). For nearly 500 years, from 240 BC to AD 225, the Parthians, whose first home had been south-east of the Caspian Sea, ruled all the territory from Mesopotamia to the frontiers of India. The Parthian Empire was a loose federation of peoples with little central control. Cities, provinces, and some small kingdoms were left to go their own ways, so long as they acknowledged the Parthians as their overlords, and paid to them all that they demanded. Zoroastrianism was the most important religion; Syriac was the language in commonest use. But in many cities people spoke and read Greek; in some there were strong Jewish communities. And of course there were many places where life and religion were on a simpler level. It was not difficult for the Christian religion to enter a land where already there were religions and cultures of many kinds.

The first Christian influence probably came from Edessa. The place in Parthia about which we know most is Adiabene, 300 miles east from Edessa across the river Tigris (map 4). Eusebius mentions Adiabene in his *Ecclesiastical History* (II 12). He quotes Josephus, saying that the Queen of Adiabene was a convert to Judaism, and that she bought grain in Egypt and sent it to relieve famine in Judea. Eusebius adds that this was the same famine for which Christians in Antioch collected money, to send to Jerusalem by Barnabas and Paul (Acts 11.29, 30). Eusebius does not mention Christians in Adiabene. He had himself visited Edessa (p. 84), but not Adiabene. Actually there were Christians there long before Eusebius's time, even just before the year 100.

One of our few sources for the history of the early Church in Parthia is the *Chronicle of Arbil*. Arbil was the capital of Adiabene. The Chronicle contains history of the Church there from AD 99 to 540. For the early period, up to 150, the writer quotes Habil the Teacher. The stories which Habil handed down are not fanciful, but seem to be matter-of-fact. They are of more than local importance, because they show conditions which may apply to other places in this wide area. The *Chronicle of Arbil* tells of:

1. One of the first converts,
2. The first martyr,
3. A highly-placed Christian,
4. Times of persecution,
5. Churches being built,
6. The extent of the Church in the year 225.

ONE OF THE FIRST CONVERTS: PAQIDA, IN THE YEAR 99

"Paqida was the son of a poor man named Beri, slave of a Zoroastrian priest." (Young 11)

Paqida was impressed by what he saw of the missionary, Addai. Notice that this is the same name as that of the missionary in Edessa (p. 85). Paquida decided to become a Christian, but his parents shut him up in a dark room. He escaped and followed Addai, who had left Adiabene and had gone to preach in villages in the mountains. He became Addai's disciple in this work.

"They say that after five years Addai ordained him and sent him home to his own people. So . . . the first Bishop, which the land of Adiabene had, was ordained by the Apostle Addai himself."

(Young 11)

THE FIRST MARTYR, SAMSUN, IN THE YEAR 123

Bishop Paqida had made Samsun his deacon. When Paqida died in 114, Arbil remained without a bishop for six years. In the year 120 the Bishop of Bait-Zabdi, a hundred miles to the north-west, came to Adiabene, travelling with a company of merchants. Hearing that there were Christians there, he secretly visited them, won their confidence, and was asked by them to consecrate Samsun as their bishop. The Chronicle continues, "Samsun began to preach in surrounding villages." Like the missionary Addai, Samsun must have found a better opportunity in the countryside. The people were fire-worshippers. Zoroastrians too regarded fire as sacred, but here was something far different. At a Spring festival a child was thrown into the fire, as a burnt-offering to the fertility spirit of the place, just like the custom condemned by the prophet Jeremiah (Jer. 19.5).

"Samsun preached to them during two years, and baptized a large number. The Christian faith spread widely in their countryside. When the nobles and Zoroastrian priests heard of this, they put Samsun in chains, tortured him severely, and cut off his head. . . . Samsun was the first martyr, who from our country ascended to heaven." (Young 376)

A HIGHLY PLACED CHRISTIAN, RAQBAKHT, IN THE YEAR 140

Raqbakht was famous and wealthy, and had been appointed Governor of Adiabene. He became an enquirer under Bishop Izhaq who baptized him, "But secretly because he feared the Emperor's displeasure". Like Addai and Paqida, Raqbakht turned to "the villages round about" as an area where he could "help the Christian faith to spread". The priests warned him, then plotted to kill him. Several of them came disguised as Roman travellers, and asked for a night's shelter. He gladly entertained them, hoping for a chance to share with them his new-found faith in the true God. *They* were hoping for a chance to murder him that night.

They were interrupted when a messenger from Ctesiphon, the capital of the Empire, galloped up. Mountain tribes had raided some cities of the north, and the Emperor commanded Raqbakht to come with all speed. So he left his guests—which meant that he escaped his murderers. Two days later the priests seized Bishop Izhaq and put him in a dark dungeon.

"They would have liked to kill him, but feared a riot and popular outcry. . . . They also feared General Raqbakht." (Young 377)

They had reason to fear. For Raqbakht heard what had happened, ordered the Bishop's release, and threatened death to any who disobeyed. The *Chronicle* calls Raqbakht "this man of God, the Constantine of his time". Alas, Raqbakht had no further chance to be champion of the Christian cause. To quote the *Chronicle* again:

"Like Judas Maccabaeus (a Jewish military leader killed in battle against the Syrians), he had given his life to his lord for his people in the fighting to which his Emperor had called him. If he had not sacrificed himself, the whole army would have perished." (Young 377)

TIMES OF PERSECUTION, IN THE YEARS 160 AND 179

"While Bishop Abraham was living among the high mountains (compare p. 93 above, "villages in the mountains"), teaching the Christian faith, the Zoroastrian priests rose against the Christians, plundering their goods and torturing them. When the Bishop heard this, he came down (to the city of Arbil) . . . and prevented the wolves from completely devouring the flock of Christ." (Young 378)

The bishop, it is added, went off to Ctesiphon, hoping to get an edict from the Emperor, to save Christians from being ill-treated by the Zoroastrian priests. The city however was in a commotion, owing to preparation for war against the Romans, so the bishop could not get a hearing. This was in 160.

The *Chronicle* says that for some years after 179, Arbil was without a bishop.

"Our brothers suffered much. Many who were young and weak in their faith, went back. For they saw their homes plundered, their sons and daughters either arrested or kidnapped. And they themselves were beaten." (Young 12)

CHURCHES BEING BUILT

The *Chronicle* mentions a church built in Arbil by Bishop Izhaq (135–148), "still standing, and called by his name", and another church which, after the death of Bishop Noah (179), was "dedicated in his name". If the Chronicle is true, these would be the earliest church buildings recorded anywhere. But we cannot be certain. The chroniclers may have mistakenly thought that churches which were really built later had been built during the lifetimes of the bishops whose names they bore. The church rediscovered at Dura-Europos (pp. 20, 21) dates from 256. It probably is a sample of what the earliest churches were like, i.e. a house, where already a congregation had been accustomed to gather, transformed into a church, but still a *house*-style and not a *church*-style building. The Edessa church (p. 85) was different. It is described, along with the royal palace, as a notable building, Indeed, it is called "the *temple* of the Church (congregation) of the Christians". So this was not a house-style building.

THE EXTENT OF THE CHURCH IN THE YEAR 225

The *Chronicle* names seventeen sees (i.e. seats of a bishop's rule) which were established before the end of the Parthian period. Then follow these words: "and there were bishops in other cities too. Nisibis and Ctesiphon (the capital) did not yet have bishops because of fear of the pagans." The seventeen places named are almost all within Mesopotamia, but one is just south of the Caspian Sea, and another is in the middle of the south shore of the Persian Gulf. By 225 the Church had extended far.

CHRISTIANS UNDER THE
SASSANID PERSIAN EMPIRE, 226

In the year 225, the Persian provinces which lay on the north shores of the Persian Gulf, and were ruled by their own king, rebelled against their Parthian overlords. The Parthian army had been weakened by wars with the Romans. The *Chronicle of Arbil* says that within that single year the Persians took over the whole Parthian empire, made Ctesiphon their capital, and proclaimed their former king Ardashir as the first of the new dynasty of Persian emperors who were called by their family name, the "Sassanid" Dynasty. The *Chronicle* says:

7.1 Constantine asked the Persian emperor to protect Christians, reminding him
that Persians had taken prisoner the anti-Christian Roman emperor Valerian. (p. 97)
This rock-carving shows Valerian kneeling before the Sassanid king Shapur I who
defeated him at Edessa in 260.

"At first there was peace for the Christians, . . . and the Gospel was able to 'send out its branches to the Sea, and its shoots to the River' "

(Ps. 80.)

This was an appropriate quotation, because the Psalmist here meant the river Euphrates.

The Sassanid Persians claimed that their Empire was the revival of the glories of Ancient Persia, five hundred years before. Sassanid Emperors were called by names famous in its history. (The name of the first one, "Ardashir", is the same as "Artaxerxes".) Zoroastrianism, the Persian religion, had already been influential under the Parthians, but now they established it as the official religion of the Empire. In foreign policy, the Persians recognized the Romans as successors to the Greeks, i.e. as Persia's traditional enemy. So there began in 225 four centuries of Persian–Roman strife: disputed territory, frontier raids, invasion, war.

Christians in Persia soon felt that they were in a dangerous position, as being a section of the people who refused to acknowledge the official religion. But so long as Christians were being persecuted in the Roman Empire, the Persian government had little reason to suspect their loyalty. The year 312 changed the situation. Constantine entered Rome under the Christian standard ("In this sign conquer," see p. 81), and Christians in Roman territory exchanged persecution for Imperial favour. The change for Christians in Persia was that now they were suspected not only because they refused to acknowledge Persia's religion, but because they belonged to the religion favoured by the enemy Roman state. Constantine himself very unwisely drew attention to this. And some Christians in Persia had not the sense to keep quiet about their admiration for pro-Christian Rome. (See Young **386, 387**.) Constantine meant well when, in 315, he wrote a long letter to the Persian Emperor in praise of his new-found faith. The God of the Christians, he said, had helped him to overthrow tyrants and to bring peace. Some of his predecessors had been persecutors, but they were destroyed by the righteous God. Constantine especially mentioned the Emperor Valerian, a persecutor of Christians (see p. 76), who had died a prisoner in Persian hands, adding "So his disgrace contributed to your glory". His letter continues:

"Imagine my joy when I heard that the fairest districts of Persia are full of those men on whose behalf I am speaking, the Christians. I pray therefore that both you and they may prosper. . . . Because your power is great, I ask you to protect them." (Young **385**)

Here was a Roman Emperor rejoicing in the large numbers of Persian Christians, and anxious that they should be protected. Naturally the Persian authorities began to suspect that Christians in Persia might welcome the protection of the Roman enemy. It is surprising that the authorities in Persia did not begin persecuting the Christians immediately.

In 337 Constantine

> "resolved on an expedition against the Persians. . . . He judged it right to take bishops with him . . . and the bishops declared their willingness to battle with him and for him, by prayers to God, from whom all victory proceeds." (38)

Constantine died before the campaign began, but the harm was done. In 339 the great persecution of Christians in the Persian Empire began.

THE GREAT PERSECUTION, 339

The first act in this new persecution was the arrest of Shimun, bishop in the capital. In his order for Shimun's arrest, the Persian Emperor called him "Head of the Nazarenes (Christians), who live in our territory, but whose sympathies are with our enemy." The bishop was to be held prisoner until he agreed that his Christian community should pay double taxation (Young **388**). For the progress of the persecution we must rely on Sozomen (see p. 89). Sozomen had read records of the Persian martyrs, and evidently these records greatly impressed him.

> "I had to decide whether to limit myself to the Roman Empire, but I thought it best to include the history of our religion among the Persians and other non-Greeks." (39)

Sozomen is the first Greek Church historian to give much attention to Christianity's eastward progress. He says that when the oppressive taxation failed to make Persian Christians forsake their religion, the Emperor

> "commanded that priests and ministers of God should be put to the sword. Church buildings were destroyed, their altar-plate was carried away to the Treasury, and the Bishop of Ctesiphon was arrested as traitor to the Empire and to its religion. In this way the Zoroastrian priests, with the help of the Jews, quickly destroyed the houses of prayer." (Young **389**)

Bishop Shimun was brought in chains before the Emperor. He stood firm, and when the Emperor said, "Take him away to the torture," he showed no sign of fear, and refused to prostrate himself. "Why do you not kneel before me, as you always used to do?" shouted the Emperor. Shimun replied, "I was not then in chains, and you were not then trying to make me desert the truth of God." "Unless you join our worship," said the Emperor, "I will destroy not only you but the whole body of Christians."

Next day was Good Friday, an appropriate day for that which was to happen. Bishop Shimun was again brought from prison to palace, and he reasoned with the Emperor in defence of the Christian faith, and showed himself determined not to submit.

"On the same day (writes Sozomen), a hundred prisoners were ordered to be slain. Shimun had to watch their execution, bishops, presbyters, and other clergy, and, last of all, he was put to death."

(Young **389**)

This was only the beginning. Persecution continued for forty years. Two of Shimun's successors as bishops in the capital were martyred. Then the bishopric was vacant for twenty years. Sozomen sums up the persecution in these words:

"I briefly state that the number of men and women whose names are known as martyred in this period has been counted as sixteen thousand. But beyond those is a multitude too great to be counted, whose names have not been listed, though Persians, Syrians, and the people of Edessa have given much care to the matter." (Young **390**)

This persecution may have surpassed any of the sufferings of the Church in the Roman Empire during the previous century.

A WORKING AGREEMENT

There were other periods of persecution in Persia, especially one under the Emperor Bihram V (420–422). Christians in Persia met their crises about one century later than those of the Church in the Roman Empire, i.e. great persecutions began in 339 and 420, compared with the Roman persecutions of 250 and 303 (pp. 74, 78). The Persian Church awaited its Constantine (p. 81), but he never came. In Persia Christianity remained the religion of the minority. But the Christian minority did come to be a *recognized* community, and did come to have, not complete toleration, but a *working agreement* with the Persian authorities.

This more settled position was reached when the Church in Persia had one of its own bishops at its head, directly responsible for Persian Christians, and becoming more and more independent of the Great Bishops of the Church in the Roman Empire. So we need to look at these Great Bishops, and at the rise of a Ruling Bishop for the Church in Persia. This may seem to be leaving our previous subject, persecution, but it may help us to understand how Christians in Persia came to better relations with the Persian State.

From St Paul's time onwards the Church in the Roman Empire was city-centred. As early as the second century, we can see Church organization being influenced by the organization of the State. For

99

example, the bishop in the capital, or "metropolis", of a province of the Empire would preside over the bishops of the province at their coming-together ("synod"). That is how the words "province" and "metropolitan", which belonged to the government of the Empire, came to be used as "Church" words, as they still are today. The Council of Nicaea (p. 139) in 325 recognized these presiding "Metropolitan" bishops and their "Provinces". It ruled that synods should be held twice a year, and that all the business of a Province needed the Metropolitan Bishop's consent. There were some bishops who had a wider authority than Metropolitans, and the Council of Nicaea made another rule, that the Church must continue to recognize three "Great Bishops":

1. The Bishop of Alexandria: he had authority over Churches in Egypt, Libya, and Cyrenaica.
2. The Bishop of Rome: no area of authority was stated, but he was the only Great Bishop for the area from Italy westward.
3. The Bishop of Antioch: again no area was stated, but he had authority in the east Mediterranean lands.

The question arises: what about Christians further east?

CHRISTIANS FARTHER EAST

Many eastern writers seem to have believed that, from the first coming of Addai (p. 93), there was always a bishop in the capital, Ctesiphon, both in Parthian and Persian periods. The *Chronicle of Arbil* is more trustworthy than such writers, saying, as we noticed on p. 95, that in 225 Ctesiphon had no bishop "for fear of the pagans". Indeed at that time it had no priest; perhaps not yet any Christians at all. About 270, so the *Chronicle* says, "a small group of Christians had begun to appear". Among them was an important Army officer, who begged the Bishop of Arbil to visit Ctesiphon. The bishop was afraid, but he came. He encouraged the few Christians, and ordained a priest for them. Then in 291, when "there was a good number of Christians, and the bishops were too far away", the Church in Ctesiphon received its own bishop. He was "a Syrian, very learned and wise", with the strange but appropriate name of Papa. (Young **382, 383**)

Papa showed his wisdom by getting to know the officials of the capital, and becoming known to the Emperor himself. The other bishops found it helpful to have a fellow-bishop who knew how to act, whom to approach, and where he could use his influence. They began to look up to Papa, and Papa himself began to realize that he had become responsible for the Church in Persia as a whole. Just as earlier, in the provinces of the Roman Empire, the Church was being influenced by the State, the bishop in the Persian capital was being accepted as chief

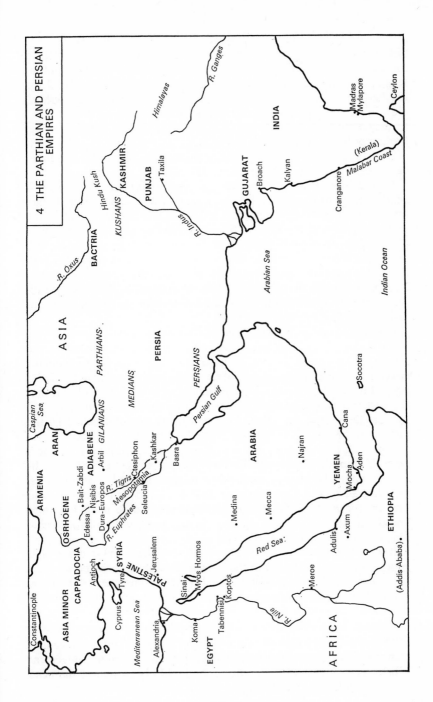

4 THE PARTHIAN AND PERSIAN EMPIRES

101

bishop. Papa wrote to the Emperor Constantine and Christian leaders in the west, suggesting that, as there were Great Bishops in Alexandria, Rome, and Antioch, another Great Bishop should be recognized for the Persian Empire. In this way Papa, the first bishop in Ctesiphon, did win recognition, if not as one of the Great Bishops (or "Patriarchs" as they would be called in the sixth century), as least as Primate, i.e. leading bishop of the Church in Persia.

Then, as we have seen (p. 98), when Shimun was Bishop of Ctesiphon, came the forty years of persecution, 339–379.

In 410 there began a great change. An Armenian bishop named Maruta came to Ctesiphon. He was a man of wide experience. He had lived in Antioch, Constantinople, Chalcedon, and had met many of the greatest bishops of the Roman Empire, including John Chrysostom of Constantinople. Now he came to act as mediator between the Roman and Persian Empires, and to help to make a treaty of peace between them. He used the opportunity to influence the Persian Emperor, Yazdgard, to order the rebuilding of churches which had been destroyed, the release of Christians in prison, and freedom for clergy and monks to travel about the country.

Maruta persuaded Bishop Izhaq of Ctesiphon to call a synod of the other bishops. Two days later Izhaq and Maruta were received by the Emperor. They read to him "a letter from the land of the Romans concerning the bishops of this place". We may guess that the letter praised the orderly life of Christians under their bishops, and said that the best way was to recognize these bishops, their chosen officers, and to trust their good discipline. As a result, the Emperor called all the bishops to his palace to hear his edict. He praised Izhaq and Maruta for bringing peace, named Izhaq as *Catholicos* (which means "whole", i.e. as bishop ruling the whole Persian Church), and commanded obedience to him. The bishops were asked to sign that they accepted this, and they all replied, "Certainly we shall do it, and sign with joy", and they instructed the Churches that "prayers should be made for kings and all who are in high positions, that we may lead a quiet and peaceable life" (1 Tim. 2.1). (Young **392, 393**)

It would be pleasant to be able to say that peace endured and that good discipline was shown in the Persian Church. But the persecution in 420 has already been mentioned, and it was accompanied by divisions among the bishops. However in 424 one further step was taken: the Persian Church declared itself completely independent of any control from the bishops of the Roman Empire. A synod of 36 bishops decreed:

"No one can say that the Catholicos of the East can be judged by those under him, or by any Great Bishop like him. Judgement belongs to Christ who has chosen him and placed him at the head of His Church." (Young **397**)

This was the way to greater security, and in that greater security, the Christian minority would grow and spread. It was monks from Persia who, two hundred years later, carried the Christian faith across Asia to the China Sea.

STUDY SUGGESTIONS

1. Draw a rough map showing the Parthian Empire and Adiabene.
2. (a) What was the capital city of Adiabene?
   (b) What was the most important religion of the Parthian Empire?
   (c) What was the language most commonly used there?
3. (a) What is the most important source-book for the early history of the Church in Parthia?
   (b) Which period does this source-book cover?
   (c) Whose stories are quoted in it for the period up to the year 150?
4. (a) What events led to Paqida's becoming first bishop of Adiabene?
   (b) Who was the first martyr in Adiabene, by whom was he martyred, and when?
5. (a) Among what kind of people were Addai and Samsun most successful in their mission?
   (b) Do you think Christian missionaries today find it easier to make converts among townspeople or country people? Give your reasons.
6. (a) Describe how Raqbakht escaped being murdered by the Zoroastrian priests.
   (b) For what reasons was he described in the *Chronicle of Arbil* as
      (i) "the Constantine of his time", and
      (ii) "like Judas Maccabaeus"?
7. What were the worst times of persecution for Christians in Parthia and Persia during the second century?
8. How did Bishop Abraham hope to save the Christians from being ill-treated by the Zoroastrian priests?
9. (a) Which church buildings are recorded by the *Chronicle of Arbil*?
   (b) What, if anything, do we know about the dates of these churches?
   (c) When were churches first built in the place where you live? (Say where you obtain this information.)
10. (a) How far had the Church in Parthia extended by 225?
    (b) Why were there still no bishops in Nisibis or Ctesiphon at that time?
11. (a) Who rebelled against the Parthians in 225?
    (b) What was the new dynasty called?
    (c) Who was the first emperor of the new dynasty? What did he call himself, and why?

12. (a) In what ways was the position of Christians in Persia changed, following Constantine's entry into Rome in 312?

(b) What two other actions of Constantine, in particular, led to renewed persecution of Christians in Persia?

13. (a) See question 1 (b) on p. 82. Compare Bishop Shimun's attitude towards the Persian Emperor with that of Jesus, Paul, and the writer to the Hewbrews, as shown in the passages quoted.

(b) Do you think that the Persian Emperors would have stopped persecuting the Christians if Bishop Shimun had obeyed Paul's teaching in Rom. 13.1, 2, instead of "resisting the governing authorities"? Give reasons for your answer.

(c) What effect might it have had on the development of the Church in Persia if the Christians there had tried to escape persecution by obeying the authorities and denying the Christian religion?

14. (a) Give two examples of ways in which the organization of the Church in the Roman Empire was influenced by the organization of the State.

(b) Give two examples of ways in which the leaders of the Church in the Persian Empire influenced the Emperors, i.e. the leaders of the state.

15. The Council of Nicaea ruled that the Church must recognize three "Great Bishops", who had a wider authority than others.

(a) In what cities were their Sees, and for what areas was each responsible?

(b) Describe the events which, according to the *Chronicle of Arbil*, led to the appointment of the first Bishop of Ctesiphon.

16. (a) What declaration did the Persian Church make in 424?

(b) What effect did this have on its development?

(c) Describe any similar declaration in the later history of the Church in Europe or elsewhere, and compare its effects with those in Persia.

CHAPTER 8

Both shores of the Red Sea

In following the spread of Christianity from Palestine eastward, we have dealt with Edessa and Armenia in Chapter 6, and Parthia, later called Persia, in Chapter 7. To the east of Persia lay India. As well as this overland route to India, there was a route from Alexandria which was almost all by water. We described it in Chapter 1 (p. 6): up the river Nile, across the desert to the Red Sea coast, by ship down the Red Sea, and across the Arabian Sea to India. On the shores of the Red Sea lay two countries whose share in the history of the Early Church we ought to notice, before we turn to India itself. These two countries are important in themselves, and important as stages towards further advance. They are Ethiopia and Arabia (map 5).

Ethiopia is important today among all the nations of the African continent, as their senior member, a truly ancient nation. The Ethiopian Church is important among all the Churches of the world because it represents the Church of the Fathers as it survives in Africa. (The Coptic Church, which means "Egyptian", is older, but for many centuries has been a Christian minority in a Muslim land.) Ethiopia is the oldest continuing Christian country not only in Africa but in the world.

Arabia is important in history as the birthplace of Muhammad (AD 570) and of Islam, the religion which he founded (AD 622), but there were Christians in Arabia centuries before Muhammad's birth.

ETHIOPIA

We noted that Luke did mention, in the Acts of the Apostles, how Christianity began to touch the African continent. Among Peter's hearers on the Day of Pentecost were men from "Egypt, and the parts of Libya belonging to Cyrene" (Acts 2.10). Perhaps they were among the three thousand people who were converted that day. And the first non-Jew whose baptism is recorded was a man of Africa, Treasurer to Candace, the Queen of the Ethiopians (Acts 8.26–39). We suggested that Luke might have heard this vivid story from Philip himself. The last words about the Ethiopian are, "He went on his way rejoicing." That "way" led 1,700 miles up the river Nile, to Meroe in what is now the Sudan, which was where Queen Candace ruled (p. 38).

The north African coast is the southern shore of the Mediterranean. This area is prominent in Roman history, and it is prominent in Church history too because it was the home of some of the earliest and greatest of the Latin Fathers. With regard to Meroe and its queen, little is known. Some of the Church Fathers guessed that the Treasurer became a missionary to his own people. It was Rufinus, about the year 400, who continued the story of Ethiopia—not the part which is now the Sudan, but the land then centred upon the city of Axum, which is the present-day Ethiopia. Rufinus was a man from North Italy, who spent twenty years as a monk on the Mount of Olives. There he did much scholarly work, especially translating Greek manuscripts into Latin, and he was generous in entertaining pilgrims. He wrote a *Church History*, and in it he included the romantic story of Christianity's coming to Ethiopia. Some Church historians seem to think that it is too good (or too romantic) to be true, but there is no reason to doubt. Rufinus himself was certain of his facts. "I am not basing this story on mere report but heard it from Edesius, who shared this experience with Frumentius, and was afterwards ordained presbyter in Tyre." Edesius was doubtless one of Rufinus's many guests on the Mount of Olives. So it seems that Rufinus's account of the conversion of Ethiopia, like Luke's story of the "Ethiopian" in Acts 8, comes to us from one of the chief actors in the story. Here is an outline of it:

Meropius, a Christian philosopher of Tyre, on the coast of Palestine (map 5), decided to visit the land of India. He took with him two boys, relatives of his, who were also his pupils. On their way home, the ship called for food and water at Adulis, Ethiopia's port on the Red Sea. Ethiopia's treaty with the Roman Empire had been broken, so the men of Adulis regarded this as an enemy ship, attacked it and killed everybody aboard it. The two boys happened to be ashore, doing their lessons under a tree. The men took them prisoner and carried them to the king at the capital city of Axum. They were well educated boys, and the king found them useful in his service. Soon he made the elder, Frumentius, his secretary, and the younger, Edesius, his cup-bearer. They became his most trusted servants. When the king died his son, the heir to the throne, was still only a little boy. The queen begged the two brothers to share the rule of the kingdom with her as regents. So government came to be mostly in the hands of the wise Frumentius. He found Christians among the Roman merchants and helped them to build places of worship. When the prince was grown up, Edesius returned to his parents and relations in Tyre. But Frumentius went to Alexandria, and reported to Athanasius the bishop,

"What the Lord had done, and asked him to consecrate a bishop for the many Christians gathered and churches built in this foreign land. And Athanasius, after careful thought, said, 'And who so fitting as yourself?' " (See Young **35**)

This was soon after Athanasius's consecration in 328. Important evidence supports this record. Ezana, King of Ethiopia, has left inscriptions in Axum, the ancient capital, which record the triumphs of his reign, 325–350. For the early victories, he gives thanks to the country's gods, but in the later inscriptions there comes a change: "Thanks be to the Lord of heaven, who in both heaven and earth is mightier than all". This shows that Ezana had become a Christian. One of his coins, with four crosses, one at each quarter, around it, is shown on p. 108. Ezana was the king in whose childhood Frumentius was regent, to whose kingdom Frumentius returned as Father-in-God, and through whose baptism Ethiopia became a Christian country before 350.

The capital of Ethiopia today is the modern city of Addis Ababa, but Axum is still the ecclesiastical capital. The church of St Mary of Zion there, a building three hundred years old, with its inside walls covered with paintings, may stand on the site of Bishop Frumentius' first church, built sixteen centuries ago.

In spite of a short break in Christian rule in the tenth century, Ethiopia can claim to be the oldest continuing Christian country in the world.

ARABIA

Christian influences entered the country of Arabia early (see map 5) From the north they came over the borders of the Persian Empire on the one hand, and of the Roman Empire on the other. In the south, Persian influences came across the Persian Gulf, and Roman influences came down the Red Sea to Arabia's tip, the Yemen.

Arabia was a country with no central ruling power. Tribes under their chieftains lived independent local lives. The same was true of Christianity's coming: there was no movement on a nation-wide scale. Records of local incidents illustrate some of the means by which the Christian religion entered and spread.

Near the Roman frontier, a warlike widow of an Arab chieftain was very much impressed by a Christian ascetic named Moses, who lived on the Roman side of the desert. She demanded, as a condition of making peace with the Romans, that Moses be handed over to become her chaplain. The record continues, "He reconciled the Arabs to the Romans, and converted many Arabs to the Faith." This was about the year 370.

Another chieftain, who was childless, consulted an Arab Christian desert-dweller and was told that, if he accepted the Christian faith, his wife would bear him a son. When the child was born, the whole tribe became Christian. Similarly with another holy man, who healed another chieftain's paralysed son.

8.1 "Ezana, King of Ethiopia, had become a Christian." (p. 107)
The crosses on coins of Ezana's reign are evidence of his allegiance to the Church.

8.2 "A Christian or pro-Christian king of Malabar, said to have died about 350." (p. 114)
The drawing is of a bronze image of Pallivanavar which was shown to the author of this book by Syrian Christians at Nilamperur in South India.

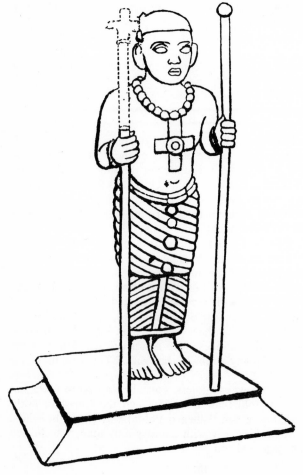

There were bishops on both Roman and Persian sides of Arabia's frontiers, but at a Synod of Antioch in 364, in the list of bishops present we find the name "Theotinus, Bishop of the Arabs".

About the year 354 we find the first mention of "Theophilus the Indian". He did not really come from India, but from an island belonging to Arabia, probably Socotra (map 5). As a boy, the Romans held him as hostage—we are not told why, nor where. Then the Roman Emperor Constantius (337–361) sent him as his ambassador, with presents, to the king of the Yemen. Theophilus, who was himself a bishop, urged the king to accept the Christian faith. The Jewish community in the Yemen strongly opposed this, but Theophilus prevailed. The king showed his sincere conversion by building three churches: one in his capital, one in Aden, the port for Roman trade, and one in the port for Persian trade, probably Cana. These churches were consecrated and adorned by Theophilus. He visited his native place, Socotra, and some other parts of Arabia, and then went to Ethiopia. (Young **36, 259**)

The letter from the Emperor Constantius which Theophilus presented to the Ethiopian king at Axum is another confirmation of the story of Frumentius. In it Constantius expresses his interest, as a Christian, in the spread of the Christian faith, but warns the king that their bishop, Frumentius, was consecrated by Athanasius, whom he called a "heretic". Actually it was Constantius himself who at this time was taking the side of the Arian heretics. Constantius had twice exiled Athanasius, because Athanasius so stoutly defended the Creed decided upon at Nicaea in 325 (p. 140).

Christians in the Yemen later suffered fierce opposition inspired by the Jews. In 523, Masruq, king of the Yemen, was the son of a Jewess, and himself accepted the Jewish faith. Najran, a town 300 miles north of Aden (map 5), was in rebellion against him. Eyewitness accounts have come down to us of what happened when the city surrendered after the king had promised that the inhabitants would be spared. All Christian males were rounded up and killed, and their church was burned. One woman, Zaruba, had gone into hiding. Hearing of the martyrdoms, she could not keep away, but went and prayed in the smoking ruin. Jews saw her there, and sent a message to the king. When she was brought before him, and refused to deny Christ, he told his men to stir up the church's embers, and throw her on the fire.

One hundred and seventy-seven wives and daughters of the Christians were assembled three days later. The General addressed them: "Jesus, son of Mary, was a mortal man. He did your husbands no good. He will do no good to you. Spit on his cross and become Jews with us." The record includes this prayer, which the women and girls prayed before they died in a shower of arrows:

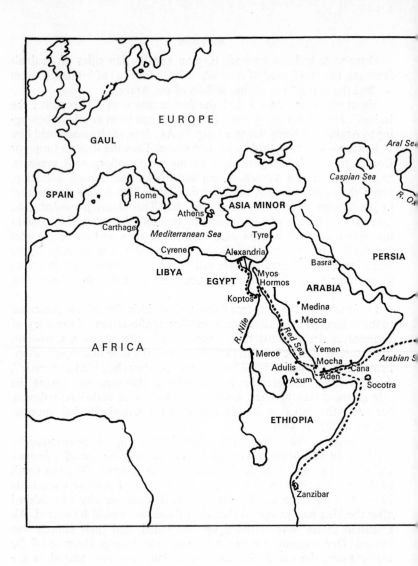

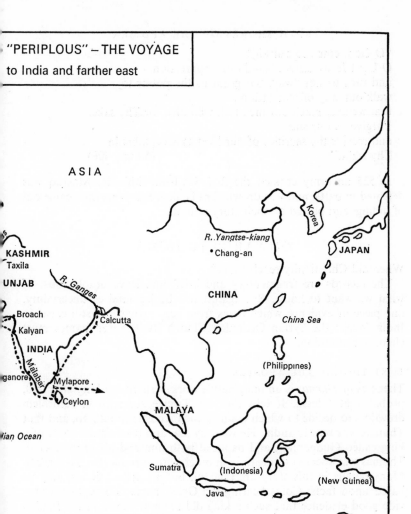

"PERIPLOUS" – THE VOYAGE
to India and farther east

ASIA

KASHMIR
Taxila
UNJAB

R. Ganges

Broach
Kalyan
INDIA
Malabar
ganore
Mylapore .
Ceylon

India Ocean

R. Yangtse-kiang
•Chang-an

CHINA

China Sea

(Philippines)

Korea

JAPAN

Calcutta

MALAYA

Sumatra
Java

(Indonesia)

(New Guinea)

"O God, come to our aid!
O Lord Jesus Christ, behold our oppression,
and turn us not away, but grant us the power to
walk our way of martyrdom,
that we may reach our men-folk who died for Thy sake.
Forgive us our sins,
and receive the sacrifice of our lives as acceptable in
Thy sight."   (Young **408**)

In 525 an army crossed the Red Sea from Ethiopia. Masruq was
defeated in battle and was drowned as he fled. Survivors then came out
of hiding, and passed on their story of it all.

ONWARDS TO INDIA

When did Christianity reach India?
   The records are fragmentary and brief, and leave untold most of
what we want to know. But against this background of uncertainty,
one piece of evidence which dates from very early times still exists in
India today: the Syrian Orthodox Church itself. Seven names must
claim our attention.

I. ST THOMAS THE APOSTLE

The *Acts of Thomas* is an imaginative work, written not long after 200,
probably at Edessa. It tells that the Twelve Apostles in Jerusalem
drew lots to decide to which country each Apostle should go, and that
Thomas was sent to India. He went by sea, and reached the court of a
king called Gudnaphar, and baptized both him and his brother Gad.
Thomas was speared to death in another part of India (see Young **23**).
Many details in this story are fanciful, but a work of fiction may be
based upon facts. Coins bearing the Greek name Gondaphoros provide good evidence that such a king did reign at Taxila in the Punjab
about the year 50. The writer of the *Acts of Thomas* knew some facts
about India. Was the coming of St Thomas a fact also? We can confidently say two things:
   (1) From the first century onwards, the journey from Alexandria
to India was being regularly made. It took about three months; some
people even went for pleasure (see p. 7).
   (2) From the second century onwards, there has been a tradition
connecting St Thomas with India. Many European travellers to India,
from Marco Polo in 1293 to Nicolo de Conti about 1430, tell of visiting
a tomb which was said to be that of St Thomas, at Mylapore, south-
west of Madras (map 5). In 1522 the Portuguese claimed to have rediscovered the tomb, and one can visit this tomb today. Members of

the Syrian Orthodox Church with one voice claim St Thomas as
their Founder.

2. PANTAENUS, ABOUT 180

We have seen that Pantaenus of Alexandria was described by Eusebius
as a philosopher-missionary who went to India (p. 42). As we have
seen, it is not known how far Pantaenus went along the Nile–Red Sea
route towards India. But Eusebius does emphasize that Pantaenus was
"trained as a philosopher", and this may suggest to us, as it did to
Jerome, that Eusebius believed that Pantaenus went to the land well-
known for its philosophers, i.e. India itself (Young **34**).

3. DAVID, BISHOP OF BASRA, ABOUT 300

A Syriac document of the seventh or eighth century says that David,
the bishop, who was an "eminent teacher, left Basra and went to
India, where he evangelized many people". Basra is on the Persian
Gulf, on the direct sea-route to India (map 5), so this reference can
mean nothing less than India itself (Young **26**).

4. JOHN THE "PERSIAN", 325

In a list of bishops who signed the Creed of the Council of Nicaea,
325, to show that they accepted it "on behalf of the Churches" in the
areas which they represented, we find this name, "John the Persian,
on behalf of (the Churches) in the whole of Persia and in the great
India" (Young **27**). The mention of Basra in the document quoted
above pointed to the sea-route. In the same way, the linking of Persia
with India in this Nicaean document points to connection over the
land frontier. Christians came eastwards to India by both routes, sea
and land.

5. THOMAS THE MERCHANT, 345

Besides these and other scattered references in documents, there is a
definite tradition among Syrian Christians in India about the arrival
at Cranganore in Malabar, now Kerala (map 5), of about four hundred
immigrant Christians from Persia led by Thomas the merchant. The
date of their arrival, 345, is claimed to be remembered from a charter of
privileges which was granted to these foreigners by the local Indian
ruler. The charter was written on copper sheets, and was in existence
till 1544. This oral tradition must be treated seriously for two reasons:
(a) Portuguese records of about the year 1600 show knowledge of this
charter and its contents (Young **409**). (b) The date 345 is at the beginning
of the Persian Church's forty years of persecution, 339–379 (p. 98).
Christians in Persia, trading by sea with south India, and knowing
fellow-Christians there, may well have come as refugees, and have been

received as a respected merchant community, just as the Parsees (i.e. "Persians") were received in India when they fled before Arab invaders in the seventh century. (See reference to "Parsee", the name for Zoroastrians in India, p. 90.)

6. PALLIVANAVAR, ABOUT 350

For the possible evidence from the same period, of a Christian or pro-Christian king of Malabar, it seems best to quote the travel diary kept by the writer of this present book. Few other Church historians, and no other Europeans, have seen this evidence. The following account of it was written during a visit to Syrian Christians in South India in 1939:

> "At the village of Nilamperur, on the eastern shore of Vembanad Lake a *mandapa* (shelter) covers the grave of a King of Malabar called Palli-vanavar, said to have died about 350. The grave was opened about 1890 by local people who hoped to find treasure. What they did dig up was a bronze image, thought to be of the king. It has since 1890 been added to the many images of the neighbouring Hindu temple. *Palli* is the word used for a non-Hindu shrine; Christians use it for 'church'. *Vanavar*, some say means 'ruler (of the *Palli*)'; others translate it 'dweller (in the *Palli*)'. One of the temple people brought out the image, and, to my surprise, put it into my hands so I could examine it in detail. The figure is $7\frac{1}{2}''$ high; has long hair done up in a knot, and covered with a headcloth; wears a *munda* (skirt) of Tamil type; he is naked to the waist. He has a necklace of 25 beads, and hanging from it a large pectoral cross, with a lotus set at its centre. Whether Pallivanavar ruled the Church, or left his palace to dwell in a church, this seems to point to a distinguished convert of this early period." (40) (See drawing, p. 108.)

7. COSMAS THE "INDIA-SAILOR",
ABOUT 525 (DATE OF HIS JOURNEYS)

Cosmas was a widely-travelled Alexandrian merchant, who became a monk, and about the year 547 wrote *The Christian Topography* ("topography" means a description of places). He said that his purpose was to answer "men who call themselves Christians, but speak against the Bible by saying that the world is a sphere". He had travelled across the world and knew that it was flat! Anyone today might be forgiven who called him a silly old man, and forgot about him and his book, though it was not until many centuries after his time that navigators like Magellan finally proved the world to be a sphere by sailing round it. But while Cosmas's chief purpose was mistaken, as he wrote he became anxious to prove the Bible right in another respect. Referring to Matthew 24.14, he writes,

"The Gospel has been preached throughout the world. I state this as a fact, from what I have seen and heard in many places." (Young **30**)

He proceeds to tell us more facts about where Christians were to be found along the trade-routes of Africa and Asia, than any earlier writer:

"In Ceylon there is a church, with clergy, and a congregation of believers, but I do not know if beyond also. . . .
Such also is the case in the land called Male (Malabar; now Kerala), where pepper grows, and in Kalliana (Kalyan, four miles from modern Bombay), with a Bishop elected from Persia."

(Young **30**)

Cosmas goes on to mention Socotra, where there are "Persian clergy and a multitude of Christians"; the whole land of Persia, with "innumerable churches, large communities, their own martyrs too"; Ethiopia and Axum; the Yemen and Arabia. (Young **5, 30, 215**)

So Cosmas not only adds details to our knowledge about India, but gives a useful summary of what we have learnt of the spread of Christianity eastwards.

STUDY SUGGESTIONS

1. (a) Tell in your own words the story of how Ethiopia became a Christian country.
(b) What was the chief city in Ethiopia when the Church was first founded there, and what is its status as a city today?
(c) In what way is the Ethiopian Church unique?
2. (a) On what evidence did Rufinus base his history of the early Church in Ethiopia?
(b) What other evidence supports his record?
3. (a) From which areas did Christian influence penetrate Arabia?
(b) In what way was the political organization of Arabia different from that of other countries at that time?
(c) Describe two incidents illustrating the spread of the Christian religion in Arabia.
4. Who was "Theophilus the Indian", and to what kings was he Ambassador?
5. In what countries today might Christian women use the prayer which the Christian women and girls of Najran prayed in 523?
6. For what reason did the Roman Emperor Constantius twice exile Bishop Athanasius?
7. The following seven people are mentioned in connection with the spread of Christianity to India:

St Thomas   Pantaenus   David   John   Thomas
Pallivanavar   Cosmas
Say in each case:
(a) Where he came from, and approximately when he lived,
(b) What his profession or occupation was,
(c) What contribution he made to the spread of Christianity eastwards.
8. What is the *Acts of Thomas*?

CHAPTER 9

Wild men of the north

After the Second World War, the phrase "One World" became a popular slogan. "One World" was used to express the interdependence of men of all nations, and this was thought to be a new fact of modern life. But we can learn about interdependence from ancient history, as well as from modern. Long ago, things happened which brought change to men's lives in one country, and another, and another, till the change became almost world-wide. Such world-wide change was sometimes caused by the movement of peoples (see map 5).

THE HUNS OF CENTRAL ASIA

Two thousand years ago, some of the wildest of wild men were the Huns, a Mongolian people, who lived to the north of the Gobi Desert, and of the highest mountains in the world, the Himalayas (map 6). These natural barriers of desert and mountains kept back the wild men from the civilized lands of China and India to the south. And the Chinese had built another barrier, the Great Wall, along 1,400 miles of their frontiers. The Huns had not learned to plough and plant. They did not build towns or even huts. They lived on a countryside until it was eaten bare, and then, with their tents and animals, moved on. It is easy to see how such wanderers became warriors. When peoples wander in order to seek pasture for their sheep or goats, the men lead or drive the animals, and men and beasts all walk. But the Huns' animals were horses, and so they rode. The Huns increased in numbers, so they moved more often, and rode more quickly. And now the sound of their coming was something to make men afraid. Instead of moving to seek fresh pastures, they rode against more settled neighbours, to rob and kill and destroy. The people of Europe called them "Huns". The Chinese called them "*Hoong*", the same word, but with a more threatening sound.

In spite of the desert and the Great Wall, some Huns moved south-east from Central Asia into China, and about AD 200 they brought to an end the civilized rule of the Han Dynasty. This was the beginning of a period of 400 years which is called in Chinese history "the Dark Ages".

In the year AD 480, some Huns went south over the Himalayas, and destroyed the Gupta Empire, under which, from AD 320, north and central India had enjoyed a golden period of civilization.

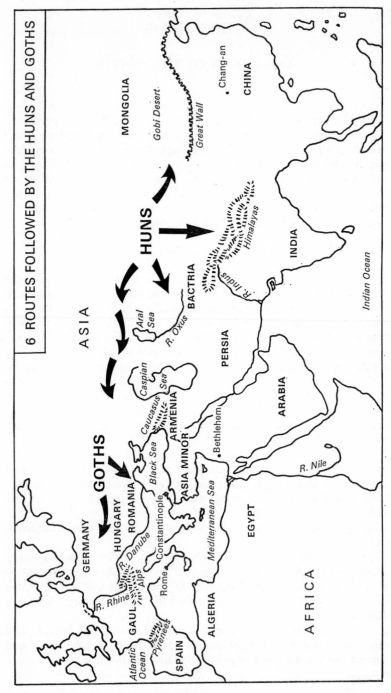

6 ROUTES FOLLOWED BY THE HUNS AND GOTHS

THE HUNS OF CENTRAL ASIA

Still more of the Huns turned west. They caught up with other wandering tribes, who had been drawn from north Europe southwards, attracted by a warmer climate, and by the frontiers of the Roman Empire, which was a land of plenty. These were Europe's "wild men of the north", the Goths. It was the pressure of the Huns coming behind them which made the Goths burst through the Roman frontiers by about the year 500. So in the west came the end of Greco-Roman civilization, and the period of Europe's "Dark Ages" began. It lasted for five hundred years.

Thus the Huns were destroyers on almost a world scale.

THE GOTHS:
GERMAN TRIBES OF NORTHERN EUROPE

Let us look a little more closely at the stages of this destruction in the west. From the second century onward, the rulers of the Roman Empire had recognized as a danger the German tribes north of the river Danube, of whom the Goths were the foremost. Some of these tribes had been allowed to settle within the Roman Empire, and had proved peaceful and submissive. More and more Goths were recruited into the Roman armies. Some Goths became officers, and in 235 one Goth who was a General became Emperor. Here were the signs of extreme danger: Gothic tribes pressing on the frontiers, and armies full of Goths set to guard those frontiers.

In the fourth century the Huns from Asia were pressing upon the lands north of the Danube which today are called Romania and Hungary (map 6). (*Rom*-ania is a relic of the Empire's name, "Roman"; Hungary, a relic of the invaders' name, "Hun".) No force could stand against the Huns' advance. Crowds of Goths fled with their families, and, in 376, asked at the Roman frontier if they could come into the Empire. Eight thousand refugees are difficult to refuse; but also, once they are in, they are difficult to settle. In 378 the refugees rose against the Roman Empire which had given them refuge. The Emperor moved his army to meet the revolt. But Roman army and Roman Emperor were destroyed. Then, worst of all, in 410 Alaric the Goth, who was in name a General in the Empire's service, besieged the city of Rome. He captured it and gave it to his Goths to loot. For eight hundred years no enemy had entered Rome's gates. This was indeed the sound of doom.

There is much in the Bible about the wrath of God, and the last judgement. When Rome fell to the Goths, Christians said (as they have said in so many crises), "This is the end of the world". Jerome (342–420) is the best example of this. He was the greatest Latin Biblical scholar. Educated in Rome, he became a monk and retired to Bethlehem, and in

9.1 "In 284 Diocletian instituted the 'Tetrarchy'—the Empire ruled by four . . .
to join in defending the Rhine–Danube frontier against barbarian invasion."
(pp. 76, 78)
A statue of the Tetrarchs—two Emperors and two Caesars, probably carved about
the year 300, is now part of the façade of St Mark's cathedral, Venice.

his monastery there translated the Bible and wrote about it—and about current events too. Though he had retired from the world, he still cared about it and wrote most vividly. In 396, he wrote:

"For more than twenty years, Roman blood has been daily shed, from Constantinople to the Alps. The Roman world is falling, yet we hold up our heads instead of bowing them down. . . . The east indeed seemed safe, but in the last year wolves were let loose upon us from the Caucasus" (he means a raid by the Huns). ". . . It is our sins which make the barbarians strong, our vices which overcome Rome's soldiers. . . . If only I had a watch-tower high enough, I would show you a world in ruins." (41)

In 409, he wrote:

"Anti-Christ is near. . . . Savage tribes in countless numbers have overrun the whole of Gaul. From the Alps to the Pyrenees, from the Rhine to the Atlantic, all has been laid waste. . . . And people who escape the sword, die of famine . . . I cannot speak without tears."
(Young **371**)

Then came the fall of Rome, in 410:

"Dreadful news from the west. Rome has been sacked. My tongue sticks to the roof of my mouth, and my voice is choked with sobs, to think that City is captive, which led captive the whole world." (42)

The fall of Rome was a tragedy indeed!

We have now to ask, and to try to answer, three questions:
1. What did the Church in the Roman Empire do about the wild men who were going to destroy that empire?
2. What (if anything) did the Church in the east do about the wildest men of all, the Huns?
3. What did the Church teach about the fall of Rome and any similar crisis which could be regarded as the "end of an age"?

THE CHURCH AND THE GOTHS

The Church had no thought-out plan for dealing with the Goths. The coming of Christianity to the Goths began through simple Christians, in a desperate situation, just going on being Christians.

In 264 Goths living in what is now Romania crossed the Black Sea and made a raid deep into Asia Minor (now Turkey), a land which was then full of churches and Christians. Greek Christian prisoners, whom the Goths captured and carried back with them, must have felt that the meaning had gone out of life, now that they were slaves of heathen barbarians. But these Christian prisoners, by their life and example, brought many of their masters to the Christian faith. One of these prisoners was grandfather of the man, Ulfilas (311–383), who was to become the Apostle of the Goths.

Ulfilas's name was really Wolf, a name which was often used for Goths (and also for Huns, see p. 121), and one which they used themselves, for they originally came from the northern forest. The German name "Wolf" sounds less fierce when it has the Greek ending: "ilas". Ulfilas's mother was a Goth, and they spoke Gothic at home, but he was given a good Greek education. At Constantinople he was made bishop: missionary-bishop to the Goths.

Ulfilas has not been given the important place in Church history to which his missionary work entitles him, because he was an Arian (p. 138). Sozomen, writing only a few years after Ulfilas's death, says this of him:

"At first he held no opinion different from the Nicene Creed. It was later that he went over to the Arian side and carried his whole people with him. . . . He had taught them the elements of religion, and a gentler way of life. They followed him, sure that he could neither do nor say anything wrong, . . . For he had faced danger for the Faith, while many Goths were still heathen. And he had taught them the use of letters, and translated the Bible into their language." (43)

Evidently Ulfilas was a practical man. At a time when the Church was full of arguments about how to express belief in Christ, he chose for his simple followers what he thought was a simpler creed (Young **260**). So he taught about Christ, not as God revealed in human life, but as a lesser god below the Great One. This was more like pre-Christian ways of thinking. Ulfilas was more capable as a do-er than as a thinker. His Arianism shows him to be a bad theologian; but his knowing what to *do* made him a good missionary.

If Christ is to come home to the hearts of any people, He must come, not as a foreigner, but speaking their language. Ulfilas saw that worship and prayers in Greek, which his people only half-understood, or the Bible read in Greek and then explained by the priest in Gothic, would not do. Bible and Liturgy must be translated. Already the Christian Scriptures had been translated from Greek into Syriac for the east; into Coptic for Egypt in the south; into Latin for southern Europe and north Africa in the west. For these wild Goths from the north, there was a special difficulty. They had a crude form of writing, but no *letters*, nothing which could be used to make a book. Ulfilas had grown up bilingual, so he knew what to do: take Greek letters to write Gothic sounds. And so he produced his Gothic Bible. It was the first book in the whole German family of languages, to which, later, English would belong.

Ulfilas knew Greek, so he knew what to do. He also knew Goths, and so knew what *not* to do. The record says,

9.2 "The Goths burst through the Roman frontiers." (p. 119)
Carving on a Roman sarcophagus shows a battle between Roman soldiers (wearing
helmets and short tunics) and "barbarian" horsemen.

"He translated all the books of the Bible, except 1 and 2 Kings, which he left out, because they are only stories of battle, and the Gothic tribes were especially fond of war, and more in need of restraint than of encouragement in this." (44)

Not all Goths who came to call themselves Christians had undergone such careful conversion to Christianity. Some immigrants into the Roman Empire accepted baptism just as they accepted other Roman ways. We even hear of some beyond the frontier, who *pretended* to be Christians, in order to get in.

Missionary work done by Christians who were not Arians is well illustrated by the greatest of Greek preachers, John Chrysostom, after he had, unwillingly, been made Bishop of Constantinople. ("Chrysostom" means "golden-mouth", a name given to him later.) John Chrysostom encouraged, and himself shared in, missions to Goths in the Roman army, and in their homelands north of the frontier. Here is part of one of his sermons which was preached in the great church in Constantinople. As well as the usual Greek congregation, John Chrysostom had invited a Gothic congregation to be present, and had arranged, within the service, for their Gothic Bible to be read for all to hear. Then, as preacher, he announced his subject: "The purpose of God for the education of all mankind", and his text, Isaiah 65.25: "The wolf and the lamb shall feed together". He said,

"The prophet is not talking about animals wild and tame. He is saying that the grace of God changes violent men to gentleness of spirit, and joins them in one society with the peaceable. And this you see here today, wild men (as they were) and lambs of Christ's flock, in one pasture, and of one fold—and, in this church, one holy table set for all." (45)

We have already remarked (p. 122) how often among the Goths the name "Wolf" appears. Listening to John Chrysostom's sermon, we may well remember Ulfilas, Apostle of the Goths, who set him the example, and whose name meant "Wolf".

THE CHURCH AND THE HUNS

In one of his letters from his monastery in Bethlehem, about the year 403, Jerome wrote,

"Every day we welcome numbers of monks—from India,
Persia, Ethiopia.
The Armenian bowman has laid aside his arrows.
The Huns are learning the Psalter." (46)

What was being done for the wild men further east? The *Chronicle of Sa'art*, written during the period 800–1300, but based on early records, tells of a revolt in Persia just before 500, which drove the Persian Emperor Qbad from his throne and from his country. Qbad fled north-east to Bactria, the region of the river Oxus, which was then occupied by the White Huns, who are also called Turks. The king of these Huns sent an army and helped Qbad to recover his throne. On his return to Persia Qbad showed favour to Christians there, because Christians among the Huns had helped him.

Some Persians, who had come with Qbad to Bactria, married and settled there. Returning to Persia in their old age, they brought more news about Christian Huns. The writer of the *Chronicle* copies from his sources the names of the narrators, and the date when they brought this news, 555. So the work described probably belongs to about the years 525 to 550:

"The Huns have learned to write their own language. This is how it happened:

In fighting with the Romans the Huns had taken prisoners. Thirty-four years later, an angel appeared to Qaradushat, Bishop of Aran in Eastern Armenia, saying, 'In answer to the prayers of the captives, God has told me to bid you to go, baptize their children, provide them with priests, give them the sacraments. And behold, I am with you, and you shall find all that you need.'

Seven of them set out through wild country, not round by the passes, but straight over the mountains, and every night they were provided with seven loaves and a bottle of water. They preached to the captives, converted some of the Huns, and translated the Scriptures into their language.

After fourteen years, Qaradushat died. His name means 'called by God'. Another Armenian Bishop, Makarios, was called to go, and went willingly, with some of his priests. They built a church of brick, planted fields, sowed vegetables, performed signs (this may mean healing), and baptized many. The chieftains of the Huns honoured them, inviting them as teachers, each to his own tribe, and lo! they are there to this day. . . . This is the time, spoken of by the Apostle, when 'the full number of the Gentiles come in' (Rom. 11.25)."

(Abbreviated from Young **39**)

This passage describes what today we should call an agricultural mission, teaching wandering tribesmen to build, to plough, to plant, and to find a better life. Less is said here about the introduction of writing and the translation of the Scriptures into the language of the Huns than was said in the case of Ulfilas and the Goths. But the same problem, the lack of letters, had to be faced, and it was solved in the

125

same way. These missionaries belonged to the part of the Church which used the Syriac Scriptures and Liturgy, not Greek, so they used Syriac letters for writing Hun sounds. Modern experts in languages of central and east Asia say that the scripts used for writing Sogdian and Uigurian show the Syriac origin of these languages and so do Mongolian and Manchu scripts, which are derived from Uigurian. Here then is another family of languages where the first beginnings of a script were for the purpose of giving men the Scriptures.

Nations of northern Europe who speak Germanic languages have reason to remember Ulfilas. People of central and north-east Asia, Turk, Mongol, and Manchu, should learn about Qaradushat. These two men were the first, and the second, Christian makers of a script. They were followed in the ninth century by the Greek Methodius, who did this same service for peoples of Slavonic speech, including Russia. And they have successors too numerous to name in the modern period, when the work of Bible translation became world-wide. In the continent of Africa alone, since 1805, work like that of Ulfilas and Qaradushat has been repeated for four hundred languages.

In many parts of the world literacy is now a national concern, and a concern of international organizations.But it is right to remember that such concern arose, first and foremost, within the world mission of the Church.

THE CHURCH AND THE END OF AN AGE

The most decisive teaching for this time of crisis, following the fall of Rome when men were thinking of the end of the world, came from the west. It came from the man who, together with Jerome (see p. 119), is counted as greatest of the Latin Fathers. This was Augustine, Bishop of Hippo, now the town of Bone, on the coast of Algeria (map 3).

After the fall of Rome in 410, refugees streamed south, through Italy and Sicily, and across to the north African coast. Volusianus, the young Proconsul, i.e. Governor, of the province, was at this time being instructed for baptism. He now asked two questions: questions which still arise in any such crisis. First, the pacifist question: Is it right for a Christian to "turn the other cheek" (Matt. 5.39) if he is responsible for the safety of a province? And second, the question of providence: "Why does God allow such things to happen?" Volusianus put this second question bluntly. He contrasted events in Rome one hundred years apart: the pro-Christian Constantine's entry of Rome in 312, and Alaric the Goth's taking of Rome in 410. "Great calamities have befallen the Commonwealth, under the rule of Emperors who were Christians. Why?"

Augustine wrote a long letter in reply to Volusianus's question. It provided the outline for a big book, *The City of God*, his most important work, which he went on writing through the thirteen years 413–426. This book is not merely one man's answer to the crisis. It has stood through the centuries as the greatest Christian philosophy of history.

While Augustine was writing, conditions in the Western Roman Empire grew worse. The Goths passed on from Italy to Spain. Another wave of barbarians, the Vandals, followed them and crossed from Spain to north Africa. In 430, while Augustine lay dying, the Vandals were besieging the walls of his city. They besieged Rome itself in 455. Augustine wrote knowing that it *was* the end of an age, but able to look into the darkness ahead with confidence. At the heart of his book is the contrast between "the earthly city, which shall not be everlasting" (the Roman Empire, or any other social order in which, for a time, the Church lives), and "the colony on earth of the heavenly Jerusalem", i.e. the Church itself, which is the City of God.

Augustine has four things to say:

1. THE CRISIS OF 410

The Christian religion did not save Rome, but it did save many who were in need. The horrors of war, Augustine says, were not new, but there was one new factor: *among the barbarians there were Christians*, who led the women and children to churches, where they would be safe from attack.

> "Whoever does not see that this is because of Christ, is blind. Whoever sees, and does not praise, is ungrateful. Whoever hinders another from praising is mad." (Young **372**)

Augustine might have claimed much more. The presence of Christians among the barbarians was later to mean that, when the Western Roman Empire ceased to be, the Christian Church remained, among western Europe's new populations.

2. SUFFERING IN GENERAL

The Christian religion does not claim that Christians escape suffering.

> "Good and evil suffer alike, but though the sufferings are the same, the sufferers are not. . . . That is not to be thought a bad death which had a good life before it. In this mortal life, a man is trained for life eternal." (Young **372**)

3. EVIL IN THE WORLD

God's creation is good. Evil exists only in man's evil will. In a world which has gone astray, God's purpose is to be found in God's people.

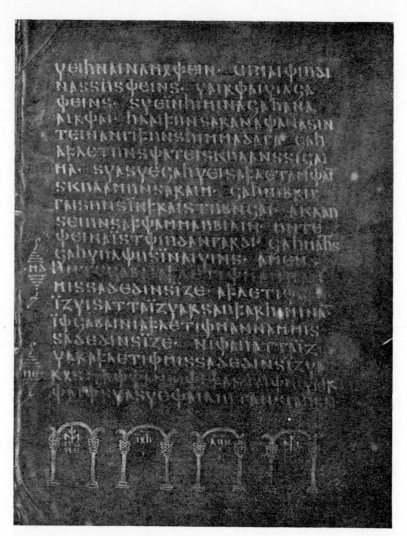

9.3 "Ulfilas translated all the books of the Bible except 1 and 2 Kings." (p. 124) The Lord's Prayer as translated into Gothic by Ulfilas is here reproduced from a 6th-century manuscript, written in gold and silver on purple parchment.

"God knew, before it happened, that man would sin. . . . For not even lions or dragons have fought with one another as men have fought. But God also knew that, from among all mankind, He would choose a People of his own, to be his children." (47)

4. THE TWO CITIES

Augustine's teaching on this subject is outlined above. He does not divide the World, as evil, from the Church, as good. He shows that the World (i.e. the secular State, or social order) has its own "good" (e.g. peace, welfare), and that the Church, while on earth, has its evil: "weeds among the wheat" (Matthew 13.25). In all that is good, the Church supports the State, keeps its laws, and co-operates in social service. Yet sometimes the Church has had to say "No" to the State, and has had to bear persecution, "until respect for its numbers, and, still more, the help of God, brought those who opposed the Church to a change of mind."

Augustine continues,

"The heavenly City calls its citizens from every race, caring nothing for differences in laws and customs and ways of life, if they do not hinder religion, the worship of the one true God. Here is truest peace, the society best ordered for enjoying God, and, in God, for enjoying one another. This peace the heavenly City while on pilgrimage (i.e. the Church on earth) enjoys already by faith, and by that faith lives righteously, since doing good towards God and towards one's neighbour does concern the peace of heaven itself." (Young **413**)

The teaching of the *City of God* is that the Church, on pilgrimage through history, is that which gives meaning to history, and that the end of its pilgrimage is *beyond* history, in the Church Triumphant.

STUDY SUGGESTIONS

1. Draw a rough map showing:
   (a) Where the Huns lived, and the areas which they invaded.
   (b) Where the Goths lived, and the areas which they invaded.
2. What do you understand by the phrase "one world"?
3. (a) What natural or man-made barriers made it difficult for the wild Huns to enter China and India?
   (b) What kind of life did the Huns lead?
   Describe in detail the life of any tribes you know which live in the same way today.
4. (a) For what reason and when did the Huns eventually enter China and India?

(b) For what reasons and when did the Goths enter the Roman Empire?

(c) What phrase has been used to describe both the period following the Huns' entry into China and the Goths' entry into Southern Europe?

(d) What were the chief differences between the Huns and the Goths?

(e) What modern country provides clear evidence that Huns from Asia advanced into central Europe?

(f) Describe one result of the Second World War and of the wars in Vietnam and the Near East in the twentieth century, which was like the result of the Huns' invasion of Europe 1,500 years earlier.

5. What important events happened in the following years?
   AD 312   AD 410   AD 480

6. What do the following names mean?
   Ulfilas   Chrysostom   Qaradushat

7. (a) What special contribution did Jerome make to the history of the Church?

   (b) For what reason has Ulfilas not been given a very important place in Church history?

   (c) List three things that Ulfilas did, which show that he was a good missionary.

8. (a) Who was Qbad and why did he show favour to Christians?

   (b) Read the extract from the *Chronicle of Sa'art* on p. 125.
   Find out if there have been any such agricultural missions to your country and, if so, in what ways they have helped the people.

9. Read Isaiah 65.25.

   (a) Give in your own words John Chrysostom's interpretation of this verse.

   (b) Which word in this verse is a link with the Goths, and why?

10. (a) Name the three earliest Christians who invented a script.

    (b) For what group of languages was each responsible?

    (c) Find out all you can about literacy work in your country, and about the agencies which are responsible for it today.

11. (a) How would you answer Volusianus's two questions:
    (i) Can a Christian "turn the other cheek" when he is responsible for the safety of other people?
    (ii) Why does God allow calamities to happen?

    (b) What four things did Augustine say in answer to these questions?

CHAPTER 10

Doctrines that matter most

ST PAUL AND THE
SHAPING OF CHRISTIAN DOCTRINE

St Paul did more than anyone else to shape Christian doctrine, to set down Christian belief *as it should be taught* (which is what "doctrine" means). He did not retire to a quiet place to think out answers to every question, and then write a textbook, *Christian Doctrine*, chapter by chapter. Shaping Christian doctrine was part of his busy life; indeed it was the heart of his missionary task.

In one of his earliest letters, Paul reminds his converts of how their Christian life began, and, doing so, he gives us an outline of his missionary preaching.

"You turned to God from idols, to serve a living and true God."
(1 Thess. 1.9)

We saw in Chapter 1 (p. 15) that many people at that time were dissatisfied with their religion, and ready for loftier ideas. That was Paul's point of contact with his hearers. There he began, calling them to turn from many gods to One, from dead idols to the living God, from false religion to one that was true. Luke, who had been one of Paul's helpers, tells of his preaching in similar words:

"You should turn from these vain things to a living God."
(Acts 14.15)

Then, after teaching about God the Father, Paul taught about Jesus Christ His Son:

"His Son from heaven, whom He raised from the dead, Jesus, who delivers us from the wrath to come." (1 Thess. 1.10)

Here were three great doctrines: Jesus as God's Son, Jesus as raised from the dead, Jesus as Saviour. And there were many other doctrines besides these. Paul's stay in one place was seldom long. He must always have wanted to go back and teach his converts more. That is why he wrote so many letters, especially if he heard of new needs arising. We can see this if we keep in mind the three doctrines already mentioned: Jesus as God's Son, Jesus as raised from the dead, Jesus as Saviour.

Paul heard that other teachers had troubled one of his congregations, saying that Christians must keep the whole Law of Moses. So Paul wrote about Jesus, and how Jesus saves. Jesus puts us right with God, not because we have rightly kept the Law, but because He has brought us into right relationship with a forgiving Father. The doctrine of salvation by grace through faith is taught in Paul's Letter to the Galatians, and (with many other doctrines too) in his Letter to the Romans.

Paul heard of doubts which troubled another congregation, doubts about life after death. So he wrote out for them something which he had told them before, the list of Christ's Resurrection appearances (1 Cor. 15.1–11; the earliest known written list). He wrote too about the Resurrection body, and ended with that shout of triumph:

"Death is swallowed up in victory.
O death, where is thy victory?
O death, where is thy sting? . . .
Thanks be to God, who gives us the victory,
through our Lord Jesus Christ."
(1 Cor. 15.54–57)

Later, during long house-arrest in Rome, Paul felt that he must write to congregations whom he might never see again. So he wrote about Jesus as Son of God: not just the Messiah, the national Saviour, whom the Jews expected, but God's Son, with God from the beginning. He wrote that Jesus, after being humbled and brought to death, was now at God's right hand, and was head of God's New Israel, the Church which is His body. These are the doctrines in Ephesians, Philippians, Colossians.

This is only part of Paul's contribution to doctrine, but it is enough to show how that contribution was made, and that it was made as part of Paul's missionary work and continuing pastoral care.

"GOD THE FATHER,
AND JESUS CHRIST HIS SON"

Origen, about the year 250, outlines a missionary method very like that of Paul. The doctrines are the same: the one true God, and Jesus God's Son. But instead of Paul's two divisions, Origen divides his first instruction into three:

"We first teach men to scorn idols and images, and after this raise their thoughts from created things to God, Creator of the universe.
By careful study of the Prophets, the Gospels, and the words of the Apostles, we prove clearly that Christ was the One foretold."
(Young 70)

We noticed earlier that the learned Origen said that Christian teachers were ready to instruct all men, even mentioning "boys and slaves and fools" (p. 44). Perhaps the third stage with its "careful study" might be too difficult for such people as these. But Origen insisted that a man could be saved from sin even if he had not much knowledge of doctrine. Origen's own work was chiefly among intellectuals. He wrote,

"We do all we can to get wise men to our meetings, and when we have many intelligent hearers we include subjects which we should pass by if we saw that those who gathered were simple folk in need of such instruction as may be called 'milk'." (1 Cor. 3.2) (48)

We shall turn to Origen's more advanced teaching later.

Another teacher who helped to shape doctrine was Lactantius, Professor of Latin in Nicomedia, where the Emperor Diocletian lived. Lactantius was dismissed when he became a Christian about the year 300, but did much to spread the faith among educated men. Writing soon after the outbreak of the last and fiercest Roman persecution in 303, he challenged the pagan authorities to use persuasion instead of force. He said they should copy the Christians' methods of religious education, and incidentally shows us how thorough such education was.

"Let them call a meeting, exhort us to take part in worship of the gods, persuade us that gods are many, show how the worship of such gods began, how this religion has been handed down to mortals, explain its source and reason, what good results from worship, what punishment follows its neglect. . . . Let them support all this by some divine evidence, as we do. . . .

If their reasoning is true, let it be made known. We are ready to hear, if they should teach. Let them do as we do, set forth a reasoned statement of the whole matter. For we do not, as they complain, entice men. We teach, we prove, we show. . . . Let them teach in this manner. . . . But if they did, even our old women and young boys would laugh at their mistakes and their stupidity." (49)

Lactantius, like Origen, outlines three stages:

"The first stage is to understand religions which are false, and to break with worship of gods made with hands. The second stage is to perceive with the mind that God is one, most high, whose power and provision made the world from the beginning, and directs the world towards a future.

The third stage is to know God's Son and Messenger, whom He sent as ambassador to earth." (Young 69)

Many Christian missionaries, from St Paul (about AD 50) to Lactantius (about 300), chose to start their teaching with the idea of God as one, living, and true. They did so, not only because many of their hearers were dissatisfied with polytheism (pagan religion with its many gods), but because the first words of the Bible are, "In the beginning, God" (Gen. 1.1). True religion does begin there.

But there was another starting point suggested in the Bible, almost a quotation of Genesis 1.1, and again a point of contact with non-Christian enquirers. It was an idea familiar from Greek philosophers, especially Plato and the Stoics: "In the beginning was the Word" (John 1.1).

"THE WORD"
THE BEGINNING FOR ST JOHN

"In the beginning was the Word;
and the Word was with God,
and the Word was God. . . .
All things were made through him. . . .
The light shines in the darkness, and the darkness has
not overcome it."

(John 1.1–5)

John, as he wrote, was thinking of how the Old Testament begins.

"In the beginning God created . . .
And God *said*," (i.e. the Word from God was)
" 'Let there be light' . . .
And God separated the light from the darkness."

(Gen. 1.1–3)

And John wrote on,

"And the Word became flesh and dwelt among us, full of grace and truth; we have beheld his glory, glory as of the only Son from the Father." (John 1.14)

John meant God's creating Word, and the Word which came to the prophets, "Thus says the Lord". That same Word in Jesus speaks directly, through a life lived among men.

But John, with these Hebrew ideas, was living in Ephesus, a Greek city. Greek thinkers would soon read his writing, and would say, "In Plato and in the Stoics, we too have an idea like that. Before the universe began, there was God alone, alone with his thought, thought coming to expression in a Word, before he made anything at all."

John may even have heard of a Jew of his own time, Philo of Alexandria, who welcomed worthy Greek ideas, and related them to Jewish teachings about God. Philo saw especially the connection between Greek thought and Jewish ideas about the Word as the power behind the world's creation, and as the intermediary between God and men.

Whether or not John himself had non-Christian thinkers in mind, the doctrine of Christ as the Word became, and has remained, the bridge by which many thinkers have crossed from non-Christian traditions to a belief in Christ.

Justin never forgot what he owed to Greek philosophy before he became a Christian (p. 13). One of Justin's sayings is, "Whatever has been rightly said among all men is the property of us Christians." As a Christian, Justin claimed all that is right in the teaching of Plato, and of Plato's teacher, Socrates, who was condemned to death in Athens in 399 BC for attacking superstition. Justin writes,

"You worship evil spirits in mistake for gods. Socrates, by true Word, tried to turn men away from evil spirits to God himself, but the evil spirits got him put to death, as godless and a blasphemer. And now they do the same to us Christians. For if there was Word present among the Greeks in Socrates, the Word took form and became man among the Jews and was called Jesus Christ." (50)

Justin recognizes that truth from God was present among the Greeks, and he hints that Christ's own death was foreshadowed in Socrates. But he saw that truth in its fullness is shown in Christ's incarnation.

We saw that the first outstanding leader of the Church in Mesopotamia was Tatian (see p. 85), to whom Christ brought "release from ten thousand tyrants", i.e. the belief that "the universe has one guiding principle". Following his teacher Justin, Tatian used the idea of the Word to explain how God and Christ belong together, though God remains One:

"The birth of the Word means sharing, but not separation. Whatever is separated is cut off from its origin, but sharing means having a task to do, along with the original. The light of the torch is not less because another torch is lighted from it. So the Word comes from the Father, without the Father having lost his Word. I talk to you, and you listen, but I am not left empty because my word has reached you." (51)

One God, and Jesus, the two great articles of belief, are not contradictory. Tatian's emphasis is on the unity of God.

Other writers used the idea of the Word vividly and poetically, without thinking of any problem about the two persons. Among them was the unnamed writer of the *Epistle to Diognetus*.

"Truly God himself, almighty, all-creating, and invisible, has sent from heaven the truth and the Word.

He did not, as men might have thought, send some attendant,

10.1 "A teacher of folly?" (p. 75)

The Pagan Greeks and Romans thought that to worship a god who had let himself be crucified was as stupid as worshipping an ass—as this mocking caricature shows. It was scrawled on the wall of a building in Rome, probably in the 2nd century, and the Greek inscription reads: "Alexamenos worships God." (Alexamenos may have been one of the imperial page boys.) But Justin and other Christian teachers showed the connection between Greek philosophy and the doctrine of Jesus Christ as the Word of God.

or angel, or one of those who manage earth's affairs, or of those entrusted with the government of heaven, but the Creator of the universe himself, by whom he made the heavens, by whom he enclosed the sea in its proper bounds . . . through whom the sun received the measure of his daily course, whose call to shine at night the moon obeys . . . He sent *him*.

Was it then, as men might think, in oppression and fear and terror? No indeed, but in gentleness and meekness, as a King he sent his kingly Son.

He sent him as God, sent him as Man to men.

As saving he sent—to persuade and not to force.

For force does not belong to God.

As calling he sent, not pursuing.

As loving he sent, not judging.

For he shall send him judging, and who shall stand his coming?"

(Young **97**)

FROM ORIGEN TO ARIUS

When we reach the third century we meet Origen, the man who did more than anyone before him to set out Christian teaching in a systematic way. He believed that the best answer to non-Christian thinkers was a full statement of Christian doctrine, expressed in words which philosophers used, but keeping close to truths from the Bible. In this book we have not space to study much of Origen's theology. But we must at least begin to understand his teaching about Christ, because in the arguments which disturbed the Church in the fourth century, both sides took most of their ideas, and some of their theological words and phrases, from Origen. Origen's great phrase about Christ is *eternal Sonship*. We must look at each of these two words:

1. *Eternal:* According to Origen, Christ reveals God as God always has been. God always has been the God and Father of Jesus Christ. "There never" (says Origen) "was, when Christ was not." He omits the words "a time (when)", because God is beyond time. He says that Christ is truly one with God, just as brightness which we see *is* light, or the stream from which we drink *is* water. These things are the same in their *being*, or substance. The Father and the Son are like that. They are the same in their being: God the Father, God the Son. Origen's word (and it is one word in Greek), is "of one substance (or 'of one being') with the Father".

2. *Son:* The name "Son" means that Christ stands second; the Father being first. Christ depends on the Father, is sent by the Father, reveals the Father, brings us to the Father. Christ is the "intermediary" between God and man. He is that which is called "Wisdom" in the

137

Old Testament, and which is called "Word" by St John, by Greek philosophers, and by Philo (in Origen's own city of Alexandria). All this is about the Son. The Father has this which is unique: beyond Him there is no other. Origen marks the difference between Father and Son in these terms; the Son is (eternally) "begotten of the Father"; the Father alone is "unbegotten".

Origen taught these two things about Christ. But his teaching, like that of many other great men, has often been misunderstood or misused, because the minds of those who came after him were not big enough to take his teaching with a two-handed grasp.

In the fourth century a great argument arose in the Church. It began in the following way. Persecution had ended, and peace had come to the Church of the Roman Empire under the pro-Christian Emperor Constantine. In Alexandria, as in every city of the Empire, thousands of people were turning to the Christian religion. The one thing they all knew was that it meant believing in one God. Alexander, Bishop of Alexandria, thought that his clergy should emphasize this point, so he gave his clergy a talk on how people can believe in one God, *and* believe in Christ. He used picture-language, as Origen had done, about the source of light and the brightness which we see, in order to illustrate that Christ, who reveals God, is one with God the Father.

Arius, one of Alexander's clergy, did not agree. The best way, Arius felt, was to teach that God the Father alone is the true and eternal God. Father and Son cannot be the same, because "Son" means that Christ had a beginning. "There *was*," said Arius, "when Christ was not." New converts to Christianity were used to the idea of demi-gods, i.e. heroes, half god, half man. Arius thought he made the Christian faith easier to understand by saying straight out that God is God, not many but One, and that Christ is neither God nor man, but Some One in between. Bishop Alexander was alarmed, and accused Arius of heresy.

Arius was correct in thinking that such teaching would be welcomed. His argument with his bishop began in a small meeting of clergy, but soon there were jokes against the bishop in the theatres, processions in the street shouted Arian slogans, songs with Arius's teaching set to popular tunes were sung by sailors loading ships and by men who rode their camels across the desert. Everyone had an opinion, and everywhere men talked about it, in shops, and markets, and at money-changers. Soon bishops from other cities were taking sides, some for Arius, some against him. The Bishop of Nicomedia where the Emperor lived, and Eusebius the Church historian, Bishop of Caesarea, both decided *for* Arius.

The Emperor Constantine was about to leave for Palestine, hoping to be baptized in the river Jordan. He decided not to go. Emperors before him had feared Christian unity (p. 74); Constantine admired it. He was now, in AD 324, the one ruler of the Empire. In deciding for Christianity he had hoped that Christian unity would help the unity of the Empire. But now the Church itself, or the Greek part of it (which was the bigger part), seemed to be breaking into two.

NICAEA: THE FIRST ECUMENICAL COUNCIL

That was why the Emperor, after sending to Alexandria to try to make peace, in 325 called a great Council of Bishops to meet at Nicaea, fifty miles east of Constantinople (map 3). 220 of them came. This was the first Ecumenical (i.e. World) Council of the Church. Eusebius, who at the Council sat on the Emperor's right, afterwards wrote about it in words full of praise:

> "The most distinguished of God's ministers from Europe, Libya, and Asia, were there . . . a Persian Bishop . . . and a Scythian (see p. 40), and even one from Spain." (52)

Eusebius continues that this fulfils the universality of the Church foretold in Acts 2.5 ("Every nation under heaven"). Eusebius, who had seen such dreadful things in the persecutions (see p. 78) only fourteen years earlier, felt that it was "like a glimpse of Christ's kingdom, more like a dream than a real event".

We have seen that doctrine was developed by the Apologists, such as Justin, Tatian, Origen, Lactantius, not by quiet thought, but in the clash of argument where Christians and non-Christians met. In the period of the Councils (325–451), doctrine developed by clash of opinions *between Christians*. We may well feel that such conflict ought to have been avoided. A Church historian named Socrates, who continued Eusebius's work, adds something like this criticism to Eusebius's glowing account of Nicaea. As soon as the bishops arrived, he says, some began to try out their arguments, and crowds gathered to hear them, as men do gather to watch a fight.

> "One layman, who had suffered in the persecution reproved them saying, 'Christ and his Apostles did not teach us skill in argument, but a mind kept simple by faith and good works'." (53)

Socrates says that, though argument continued for thirty years after Nicaea, it was like a night battle in which no one sees clearly the position which he attacks. He says that both parties really believed in one God in three Persons, but neither of them knew how to say so.

At the end of his *Church History*, Socrates wishes

> "Peace to Christians and to churches everywhere, with cities and nations, then those who want to write church histories will find

nothing to write about, even as I should not have been able to write
seven books, if trouble-makers had chosen to keep quiet." (54)

The creed of Nicaea, 325, sets out right belief in the Three Persons
of the Trinity, centring attention on the Father and the Son. The key-
word of the whole statement is that the Son is "of one substance
(or 'being') with the Father". This is followed by the clause, "Who
for us men and for our salvation, came down from heaven, and was
made flesh, was made man". This means that Christ is fully God, and
Christ is truly man.

THREE VIEWPOINTS:
ANTIOCH, ALEXANDRIA, ROME

Earlier the problem had been how three Persons could be One God.
There now remained the problem how two natures (God-nature and
man-nature) could be together in one Christ. Each of the three Christian
centres, (1) Antioch, (2) Alexandria, (3) Rome, had its own theological
point of view. In this brief summary of the argument we shall attach
one word as a label to each centre, and briefly say (a) why this point of
view was held, (b) what its effects were on people's thoughts about
God and man, and (c) what its effects were on thoughts about the
Person of Christ.

I. ANTIOCH. THE WORD IS "SEPARATION"
Jewish influence on the Church at Antioch had been strong.

Taught by the Jews, the Christians of Antioch kept their thoughts
of God and man in reverent separation. God made man in His own
image. Man sinned, and lost God's image. God began a new creation,
and sent a Second Adam, Jesus, who this time was strengthened by the
Word planted in him. All is two-fold—Creator and creature, God and
man. In thoughts about Christ, the two natures were kept separate:
God-nature and man-nature side by side. The Christians of Antioch
believed that Christ came to earth as a man, but that the significance
of his life was that God lived in him.

2. ALEXANDRIA. THE WORD IS "UNION"
Greek philosophy had a strong influence in Alexandria, and the aim
of most Greek philosophers was union with God. (See p. 60 for
Clement's ideas of philosophy as "educating the Greeks to bring them
to Christ".) Athanasius, who was at Nicaea in 325 as secretary to Bishop
Alexander, and himself became bishop in 328, wrote a book called
The Incarnation, in which he made this statement about union with
God: "The Word became man, that we might be made God." In the

Alexandrians' thoughts of Christ, the problem of the two natures was solved by *union*: God-nature and man-nature joined together made the God-man, who had divine humanity.

Each of these two different ways of thinking could lead to difficulties. Nestorius had been educated and had served as presbyter in Antioch before being made Bishop of Constantinople in 428. His enemies were able to get him charged with heresy and deposed by the Council of Ephesus in 431, because he opposed terms like "Mother-of-God" as irreverent, and because he seemed to speak as though Jesus was two separate persons, the man whom Mary bore, and the divine One who lived in him. Of course Nestorius did not believe in two persons. Nestorius himself said, "I separate the natures, but I combine the worship". A more positive statement of this way of thinking was made by Bishop Theodore of Mopsuestia, who explains Christ's "taking the form of a servant" in these words:

"He clothed himself with our nature. He who put it on was God. That which He put on was man." (See Young **268**)

Eutyches on the other hand represents an extreme of the Alexandrian view. He said, "After the union (of divine and human in Christ), I confess one nature only, the divine". One who opposed this view said that if Christ was not a real man, then He could not be man's real Saviour. The fourth council was called at Chalcedon (see map 3) in 451, to consider and condemn this extreme point of view.

With the sharp rocks of these differences ahead, how could the Church escape "shipwreck of the Faith"? A steadying influence came from the west, from Rome, the third centre.

3. ROME. THE WORD IS "MEDIATION", WHICH MEANS "STANDING BETWEEN"

The leaders of thought in the west had been practical. They had started, not with the inner life of God, but with the actual life of men, thinking about man as a sinner and how he may be forgiven.

They saw that man stands before God as a debtor who cannot pay. Christ comes, as God-made-man, and pays the debt for him. Christ is Mediator: as God, He *can* meet the need; as Man, He stands where the need is. Because He is both God and man, He can be Saviour. From Tertullian of Carthage to Augustine of Hippo, Christians in the west had been taught to think in this way.

Leo, Bishop of Rome, could not go to the Council at Chalcedon, but he sent a letter. It was written in Latin, for Leo knew no Greek. Translation generally weakens a statement, and another person's reading weakens it again. Yet Pope Leo's letter excited the Council; the bishops rose and shouted, "Peter has spoken!"

10.2 "The most distinguished of God's ministers from every nation under heaven were there." (p. 139)
Michael Damaskinos painted the bishops at Nicaea many centuries after the Council took place. But his picture clearly shows the "clash of opinion" between them.

THE CHALCEDONIAN DEFINITION

Leo is one of only two Popes whom history calls "the Great". He was great when he helped to save Rome from the Huns in 425, and from the Vandals in 455. But another of his successes was when he helped to save the Greek part of the Church from its divisions. His letter (or Tome, as it has been called) influenced the form of the Council's findings. These were called, not the "Creed", but the "*Definition*" of Chalcedon.

"Definition" seems a strange word to use. To define means "to describe accurately". The question which was being discussed was, "How can Christ be both divine and human?" The Fathers at Chalcedon did not mean that they had answered that question with accurate description. But "to define" can mean "to make more definite". And with regard to the question, they had done just that. The answer given at Chalcedon leaves aside the question *how*, but states more definitely that Christ *is* both divine and human, in this way, in that way, and in every way. The Fathers were anxious only that nothing should be left out.

"Our Lord Jesus Christ is one and the same Son, perfect in God-head, and perfect in manhood, truly God, and truly man, of a reasonable soul and body; of one substance with the Father in God-head, of one substance with us in manhood, like us in all things except sin; in the last days, for us and for our salvation, begotten of the Father before the ages as to the Godhead; born of Mary the Virgin, Mother of God, as to the manhood; one and the same, Christ, Son, Lord." (See Young **284**)

We may ask whether this century-and-a-quarter of argument (325 Nicaea–451 Chalcedon) did anything to make it easier for people to believe in Christ and in God? The student of history may sometimes feel like saying "No", when he remembers how Socrates described some of the quarrels: like night-fighting, in which no one sees his opponent clearly, both sides believing alike but unable to say so. Perhaps some of us, as we finally think about Chalcedon, may say, "Yes". The Chalcedonian Definition does not solve the mystery, but does define it, *and calls us to lay hold on our Christian inheritance with a two-handed grasp.*

STUDY SUGGESTIONS

1. (a) Which *three* of the following words have the same or nearly the same meaning as "doctrine"?
   doctorate   teaching   preaching   document   tenet   concept

(b) Look up in a dictionary the two words "doctrine" and "dogma", and then in your own words briefly explain the difference between them.

2. Read the following passages from the record of Paul's teaching and his letters.

(a) What three important doctrines about God the Father do they contain?

(b) What three important doctrines about Jesus do they contain? Give the references in each case.

Acts 13.23; Rom. 8.3, 4; Rom. 15.8, 9; 1 Cor. 8.4–6; Eph. 2.4–6; 1 Thess. 1.9, 10.

3. To what kinds of people did Origen chiefly preach?

4. Read Gen. 1.1–5; John 1.1–5; John 1.14.

(a) What important Christian doctrine do we find in all three passages?

(b) In what way or ways was this doctrine related to the ideas of the Greek philosophers?

5. When and where did each of the following live?

Justin Tatian Origen Lactantius Arius Nestorius

6. (a) Justin said: "Whatsoever has been rightly said among all men is the property of us Christians."

What is your opinion?

(b) What particular doctrine did Tatian teach?

7. (a) Outline briefly in your own words the three "stages" in Christian education as taught by Lactantius.

(b) Lactantius was Professor of Latin in Nicomedia but was dismissed when he became a Christian. Where and in what circumstances today might a school or university teacher be dismissed for being a Christian?

8. (a) Which great teacher described the nature of Christ by the phrase "Eternal Sonship"?

(b) What do you yourself understand by this phrase?

9. (a) In what chief way did the teaching of Arius differ from that of Origen?

(b) For what reason, do you think, did people accept the teaching of Arius?

(c) What effect did his teaching have on the Church as a whole?

10. (a) In what year was the first ecumenical council held, and where did it take place?

(b) For what reason was it held?

(c) What was its most important result?

11. (a) Describe briefly the three theological standpoints represented by the three great centres of Christian thought in the fourth and fifth centuries AD:

Antioch   Alexandria   Rome

(b) What was the chief difference between the ideas of Athanasius about God, and those of Nestorius?

12. (a) What was the "Chalcedonian Definition"?

(b) What question was it supposed to answer?

(c) Express that answer briefly in your own words.

(d) What did the bishops at the Council of Chalcedon mean when they shouted "Peter has spoken"?

13. (a) By what means do the Churches today decide how to answer questions about the nature of God?

(b) What would you reply to someone who said that the Churches' traditional doctrines about God and Christ need to be drastically changed in the light of modern scientific and technological discovery?

CHAPTER 11

The coming of the monks

THE CALL TO LIVE APART

The word "monk" comes from the Greek *monachos*, which means "one who lives alone". That is how, in Egypt, soon after AD 250, this movement started: men began to go out from village or town to live in the desert, alone. Some, as we shall see, thought it better to live in a religious community, not alone, but apart from ordinary people. So perhaps we should explain "monk" as "one who lives apart", separate from the world.

Why should Christians feel that they had to leave the ways of ordinary life? Such a call to separation is to be found in many religions. The *Sadhu*, or "holy man" living in forest or mountain, was and still is a familiar figure among Hindus in India. Buddhism, which began in India 500 years before Christ and spread south-east across Asia, teaches faith in the "three refuges": the Buddha, the Doctrine, the Order. The Order means the whole body of monks, and this is not merely a movement within Buddhism, but one of the three essentials of that religion.

The religion of the Jews, within which Christianity arose, may seem quite different. The Old Testament teaches men, not to leave the world, but to see God's blessing in flocks and herds, wives and children, and God's reward of the righteous: "In all that he does, he prospers" (Ps. 1.3). Yet there were Jewish communities, such as the Essenes from about 200 BC onwards, and the Qmran community which had the Dead Sea Scrolls, whose members were very like monks. John the Baptist, last of the prophets and forerunner of the Christ, lived alone on the edge of the desert (Luke 3.1–6).

Jesus was so different from John the Baptist that some people asked the reason for this (see Luke 5.33). Others, contrasting Jesus with John, called Jesus a glutton and a drunkard (Luke 7.34). Yet Jesus blessed the poor (Luke 6.20), was homeless (Luke 9.58), and called His followers to be prepared to leave all they had (Luke 14.26, 27).

The passage in the Gospels which has most often moved men to seek a way of more complete devotion to Christ, is: "If you would be perfect, go, sell what you possess, and give to the poor . . . and come, follow me" (Matt. 19.21).

The early Church, in the period of persecution, knew itself to be separate from, and opposed by, an evil world. For this reason, fellowship within the Church was close, discipline was strict, and standards were high. Tertullian says:

> "Trust in God is strongest when persecution breaks out. The Church is hushed. Church members are full of zeal. They keep the fasts, attend the services, are humble, kind, and loving. . . . All compromise is idolatry. To refuse martyrdom is to deny Christ." (55)

Here was a more complete devotion.

In the fourth and fifth centuries came two changes, one change in the world, the other change in the Church. (a) The world, especially the western Roman Empire, seemed to be coming to an end (pp. 126–127). (b) The Church became accepted by the world, and (some felt) became worldly (p. 82). These changes encouraged the monastic movement. Some men left the world because they despaired of it; others left the worldly Church for the more devoted life of the monks.

We shall look at the coming of the monks in Egypt, among the Greeks, in the east, and in the west.

EGYPT 1:
ANTONY (251–356), AND THE
DESERT FATHERS, LIVING ALONE

It is right to begin with Antony, because the great Bishop of Alexandria, Athanasius, who knew him well and wrote his Life, calls him "the model for monks".

Antony was born at Koma, a small town 240 miles up the Nile (map 7). When he was eighteen, his parents died, leaving him their farm. Six months later, he heard the Gospel read in church, Matthew 19.21 (p. 147). The words came to him as Christ's command, and he obeyed. Then, homeless, he went to live among the graves outside the town. Later he moved to the desert beyond, where he found shelter in a ruined fort. He lived there for many years, most of the time alone.

Everybody believed that the desert was the home of evil spirits, and Antony often felt powers of evil around him. Homeless, hungry, short of sleep, missing so many of the things which make a man's life human, i.e. different from the life of an animal, he even *saw* the devils in dreadful shapes. But he was far from being mad. In the desert he gained a strength of character, upon which others could lean.

During the last Roman persecutions (311, p. 78), when the Bishop of Alexandria was martyred, Antony appeared in the city. He seemed like a messenger from another world, beyond the power of the persecutor, beyond the fear of death, and he brought courage to the Church. Men came to him in the desert and begged him: "Speak a word to me,

Father, that I may live." And Antony spoke. He had had little education, but he was wise. They brought the sick and devil-possessed to him. "Pray to God", said Antony, "not to me." But sometimes it was Antony's word which brought the cure. This man of the desert several times wrote to the Emperor Constantine about Church affairs, and the Emperor wrote back. "I visited Antony often," says Bishop Athanasius himself. And later, when there was some opposition to the Nicene Creed, the bishop sent for Antony to come to Alexandria again, and took Antony with him visiting the Churches. Sozomen says,

"Everybody felt honoured to see him, listened eagerly to his words, was persuaded by his argument. But he preferred to be unnoticed. 'Fishes', he said, 'are made for water, and the desert is the place for monks.' " (Cf. p. 24.) (56)

Even in the desert Antony had "kept his manners and was not rude". He kept his humility too; as a layman he treated "even the youngest deacon with respect".

More and more men went to him to learn about the life of prayer, and many stayed near him in caves or huts, or in the shelter of a rock, living alone, but with Antony as spiritual Father.

Later he pushed further into the desert and settled in an oasis within sight of the Red Sea which is still called Antony's Mount. And there at the age of 105 he died, attended by two of his disciples.

" 'The sheepskin, on which I am lying, give to Athanasius the Bishop. He brought it to me when it was new. . . . And you take my hair shirt' (all the property he had). 'And farewell, you whom I love dearly. For Antony is going, and will not be with you in this world any more.' And stretching his feet a little, he looked joyously on death." (57)

EGYPT 2:
PACHOMIUS (290–346), AND MONKS
WITH COMMUNITY, RULE, ORDER

We know less of Pachomius than of Antony. Pachomius had no one close to him in space and time to write about his life. But we know more of Pachomius's organization, because that was his gift. Antony's monks were individuals, with little connection between them except love towards Antony and some obedience to senior monks. Pachomius added, for his own monks, a *Community*, a *Rule*, and an *Order*.

COMMUNITY

As a youth, Pachomius was forced into the Roman army. He found comfort and help from village Christians, and when he became free he asked for baptism. An old monk taught him prayer, fasting, and obedience. Then one day at Tabennisi, an island where the river Nile turns to the north-west, Pachomius heard a voice saying, "Stay here, and men will gather to become your monks." Sozomen praises him as "a man who loved men, and was beloved by God". He not only loved men, but knew how to deal with them. He was soon Abbot (i.e. "Father") of a monastery of 1,300 monks.

RULE

The Rule, i.e. the instructions which Pachomius laid down for the life of the monastery, was inscribed on a copper plate. The monks said that it had been handed to Pachomius by an angel from heaven. We do not know what was on the copper plate, but we do know his monastery's regulations. Here is an outline of them:

A man wishing to become a monk must apply to the gate-keeper. He was then lodged in a guest room near. For some days, while he was learning the "Our Father" and some Psalms, some of the monks found out all they could about him. If they considered him suitable, he was taught the Rule, given a monk's clothes (see below), and introduced to the ways of a monk.

Each monk had his own cell, or small room, but no lock on the door. The clothes were three shirts, two caps, and a head-cloth (for shade from the sun), a leather coat (for winter warmth), shoes, and belt.

Men in one lot of cells formed a group, under one head-man. Each group had its own trade (making reed mats, weaving, laundry, making clothes or shoes, carpentry). Each group would take its turn to serve the whole community in farm, kitchen, hospital, or marketing. There were two meals a day, taken by the group together, but in silence, at noon and evening. The monks did most of the work alone in their cells, and most of their praying also. But before dawn, and again as darkness fell, the group came together for worship. Wednesday and Friday were fast days (see p. 31), and on Sunday the whole community came together for Eucharist. (Young **424**)

ORDER

By "order" we mean the organization of all Pachomian monasteries together. Sozomen sums up Pachomius's success in these words:

"By adopting this Rule, his monks became famous, and increased in numbers so vast that they reached seven thousand, all regarding the monastery at Tabennisi as their Mother." (58)

There were, in 356, nine monasteries and two nunneries in various parts of Egypt. So Pachomius died, not only Abbot of a monastery, but Head of a whole Order of monasteries.

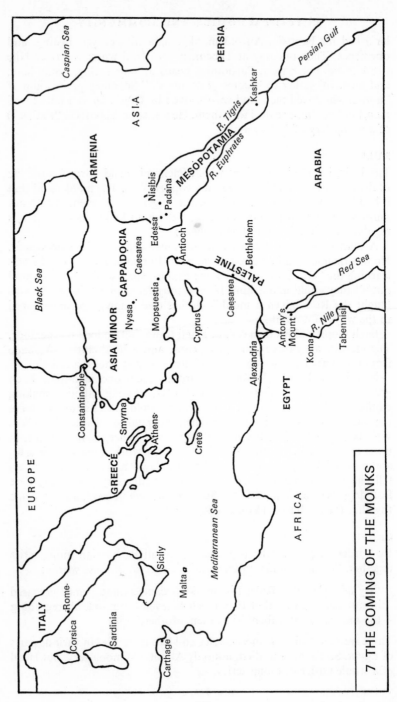

7 THE COMING OF THE MONKS

THE GREEKS:
BASIL OF (CAPPADOCIAN) CAESAREA
(330–379)
AND MONKS SERVING THE NEEDY

Most monks in Egypt were simple men, Coptic-speaking, and of little education. Basil belonged to one of the most highly respected families in Cappadocia, which was also a devoted Christian family. His sister, Macrina, after the death of her betrothed, had decided not to marry, and had given herself to the religious life. Then (to quote an account by another member of the family, Basil's brother Gregory of Nyssa),

"The great Basil returned from study abroad" (i.e. in Constantinople and Athens). "He seemed so proud of himself, but Macrina took him in hand, so that he left worldly glory, turned from fame as a speaker to this busy life" (i.e. a monk's), "where a man toils with his hands, and gave up his property, lest it should hinder the good life."

(Young **81**)

Monks often linked together work and prayer, and it was hard manual work that they did. Basil visited the Desert Fathers in Egypt, Palestine, Syria, and Mesopotamia, and learned much that helped him in founding his own religious communities (Young **81, 82, 426**). His Rule became, and still remains, widely influential in Greek monasteries. It sets out the religious life in poverty (i.e. without personal possessions), chastity (which includes celibacy), and obedience; the times for prayers through day and night, the work to be done with the hands. Basil not only believed, as did Pachomius, that life in community was better; he regarded the solitary monk (e.g. of Antony's tradition) as mistaken.

"Living alone, a man seeks only his own salvation, which is contrary to the law of love. . . . He has no one to correct his faults. . . . God has made us, like the different parts of a body, to need each other's help. . . . He who lives for himself, may have a precious gift, but he buries it. Whoever reads the Gospel (Matt. 25.25, 26), knows the danger of doing that. Men in community share each other's gifts. . . . How can anyone be humble, merciful, or patient, unless someone else is there? Whose feet will you wash, whom will you serve, how can you be least of all, if you are alone?" (59)

Still more important, Basil linked the monk's life with service of the needy. Basil tells us that after he became Bishop of Caesarea he provided a series of great buildings just outside the city, for the work done by his monks. There was a guest-house for travellers; a hospital with

151

doctors, nurses, and attendants; a poor-house where men could learn a trade; and even a home for lepers. There were so many of these buildings that people called them "the New City". Some people thought his plans extravagant, but this is how Basil's closest friend Gregory of Nazianzus thought of them:

"Basil has persuaded the rich really to store up treasure in heaven. Here you may see religion dealing with misfortune and disease. . . . No more will you meet lepers, cast out, dreaded but not pitied; half-dead already, singing their sad songs, if left with any voice to sing. . . . Basil has greeted them as brothers, come to look after them, and brought the leaders of society to follow his example. . . . Cooks and feasts, carriages and flowing robes—the Bishop cared for none of these. He did care for the poor. He cared for following Christ, in cleansing the leper—not talking about it, but doing it." (58)

THE SYRIAC-SPEAKING EAST:
EPHREM OF NISIBIS AND EDESSA
(308–373)

When Basil wanted to learn how to be a monk, he went not only to Egypt, but to Syria and Mesopotamia (map 7). Both of these were desert lands like Egypt, and Christians there had been early influenced by the Desert Fathers. Basil wrote about monks he met there:

"I admired their self-control, their hard work, their frequent prayers, their little need of sleep . . . I prayed that I might imitate them."
(Young 82)

Sozomen names nine men of Nisibis, who became monks and were called "the shepherds", because they lived in the open on the mountains,

"with prayers and praises according to the laws of the Church" (i.e. at the set times for prayer). "They had no bread nor meat nor wine, but at meal-times went out with a sickle, and cut grass to eat."
(60)

But he says that the first monk of all in these countries was Aones:

"Aones had a monastery in Padana, which was the very place (Paddan-aram, Gen. 28.2), where Jacob, grandson of Abraham, met the girl Rachael, whom he married. It is said that Aones was the first to bring to Syria the idea of living apart, the strict life, just as Antony brought it to Egypt." (61)

In the place where Jacob found, not one wife, but four, Aones and his monks, by contrast, were celibate.

Most honoured of all Syriac-speaking monks was Ephrem. He was born in Nisibis:

"My parents" (he says) "trained me in the fear of the Lord. They were confessors" (i.e. sufferers in the persecution). "Yes, I am related to martyrs." (62)

When the Persians took Nisibis in 365, Ephrem moved to Edessa. He wrote on the Bible, Christian doctrine, the Christian life, and also a vast number of poems and hymns. He began writing in verse to counteract the influence of heretics who were spreading their teaching in songs (p. 138), which even children liked and learned. Ephrem decided to compete with them, and soon he drew the crowds to Church, because his verses were in beautiful Syriac, set to popular tunes, and were sung by a choir of girls preparing to be nuns, whom he had taught to sing.

Sozomen says that Basil "greatly admired" Ephrem, and we know it from Basil's own letters. Ephrem was not only a great writer, but a monk of strict life and full of good deeds. Speaking of the strict life, Sozomen says that Ephrem "kept even from the sight of women". The girls' choir must have been an exception, and we hear of another exception, when Ephrem rebuked a woman who stared at him.

"When you meet a monk," (he told her) "your eyes should be on the ground." "No," said the woman, "*your* eyes on the ground, since man was made from the dust of the ground, but 'the rib taken from the man God made into a woman' (Gen. 2.22). So *my* eyes can look on the man!" (64)

Ephrem had a sense of humour. He wrote the story of this conversation in one of his books, and people liked it.

Sozomen tells of one good work of Ephrem's which Basil (if he heard of it) would greet with a cheer. Famine came to Edessa, and Ephrem came out of his cell to rebuke the rich for leaving the poor to die. "We would gladly give our money," they answered, "but we know no one whom we can trust to distribute food to the needy." "Then what about *me*?" said the monk. The rich did give to Ephrem, and he had three hundred beds set up in the town's public shelters, and he himself, day after day, was busy serving those weakened by starvation. A few days after the famine ended, Ephrem died. "He was only in deacon's orders," says Sozomen, "and never became a priest, but he is remembered among the best of good men."

We must note two more points about Syriac-speaking monks.

First, the development of *communities*, living under a monastic rule. What Pachomius did for Coptic monks and Basil for Greek monks in the fourth century, did not happen in the Syriac-speaking part of the

THE COMING OF THE MONKS

Church until the sixth century. This was the work of Abraham of
Kashkar, 502–596, whose home monastery was not at Jacob's Paddan-
Aram, but at Abraham's Ur of the Chaldees.

Second, monks as *missionaries*. Sozomen remarks upon the long life
of many of these eastern monks:

> "God added to their years for the sake of religion. He used them to
> lead nearly all the Syrian nation, and many of the Persians, to the
> true Faith." (65)

The monks were the missionaries of the Church's eastward expansion.
Monks from Persia completed the progress across Asia, arriving at
China's capital in 635.

THE LATIN WEST: JEROME (342–420)

Ephrem once said,

> "Through all my life, I have never spoken ill of anyone, except to
> dispute with those who deny the Christian Faith. Disputes were
> sometimes necessary, for if a wolf approaches the fold, the dog must
> come out and bark, or be beaten by his Master." (66)

Jerome could not have said that. He loved an argument, was always
ready for disputes, and made enemies everywhere. Reading his letters,
we may wonder why we should call him "Saint". But if we read on, we
begin to feel sorry for Jerome. He caused trouble because he lived in
troubled times, and often his own heart was not at peace. Here are
three of his troubles: (a) the choice—Cicero or Christ? (b) the problem
of the worldly Church; (c) the tragedy of the falling world.

(a) CICERO OR CHRIST?

These words may seem strange, but the trouble is familiar to many
students today in lands where translators have not yet produced a Bible
of good literary style. That is how men of keen literary taste felt about
the Latin Bible then. Jerome tells this about his own youth:

> "For the Kingdom of God's sake I had already left home, parents,
> relations, the dainty food to which I was accustomed. But I could
> not part with the books which I had collected at Rome with great
> care and toil" (He mentions Cicero and other Latin classics.) "When
> I read the Bible, the style seemed rough and put me off. I failed to
> see the light, and blamed, not my own blind eyes but the sun." (67)

Then Jerome had a serious illness, during which he had this dream at
Antioch in 373:

"I was caught up before the judgement seat and God the judge. The light there was so bright that I dared not look up. 'Who are you?' —'I am a Christian.'—'You lie. You are a disciple of Cicero, not of Christ, because where your treasure is, there shall your heart be also' (Matt. 6.21). I was ordered to be flogged. Was it only a dream? I swear that my shoulders were black and blue when I awoke.

After that I read God's Book with a greater zeal than the books of men." (67)

Of course Jerome did not throw away his library, but he did give his life to study of the Bible. (See below, p. 158.)

(b) THE WORLDLY CHURCH

In 382, after experience as a monk in the Syrian desert, when he learnt Hebrew to help his Bible studies, Jerome arrived in Rome. From his years as a student there, he had loved and honoured the tombs of the martyrs. He found that Pope Damasus was adding marble inscriptions to these tombs, and doing much to collect and preserve historic records. The Pope welcomed Jerome as a man of learning, and asked him to revise the Latin Bible.

Jerome must have felt uneasy as he read the account, written by a non-Christian, of the riots which occurred when Damasus was elected Pope and his supporters clashed with those supporting his rival:

"They found 137 bodies of those killed in the church—*where there is a congregation for Christian worship.*" (68)

And when he heard the sneer of a non-Christian Senator: "Make *me* Bishop of Rome, and I will become a Christian!" he must have felt like asking: "Was the highest office in the Church a prize to be fought for?"

Jerome wrote vividly, if cruelly, about Rome's worldly clergy. He tells of a priest who visits a wealthy lady of Rome's aristocracy:

"On leaving, he spreads out his hands, not (as you might think) to give the blessing . . . but only to receive his fee for the call. . . . She, seeing the priest so dependent, is exalted with pride. After eating too much supper, she goes to bed to dream of the Apostles."
(69)

Some clergy, he says, used perfume, curling tongs for their hair, rings on their fingers—"more like bridegrooms than clergymen".

Pope Damasus was seventy-eight years old. Jerome was so much in favour that he believed Damasus wanted him to be his successor. Could a monk become Pope? Why not? Jerome was the most learned man in Christendom. A few years before, when Basil's friend Gregory (p. 152) saw the chance of becoming Bishop of Constantinople, he had turned

away, saying, "Give me my desert, my country life, and my God."
But Jerome might bring the spirit of the desert to the See of Peter and
the capital of the West.

In 384 Pope Damasus died, and the next year, instead of succeeding
him, Jerome left Rome never to return. It was a triumph for the worldly
clergy. But even in retreat Jerome struck a blow against worldliness,
which set all Rome talking.

His greatest influence had been over a group of ladies in one noble
household. *They* did not "dream of the Apostles", but listened and
learned eagerly as Jerome taught them to study the Bible in both
Hebrew and Greek, to serve the poor and needy in the city, and to live
(like nuns) according to a strict rule. Two of these women, the widow
Paula and her daughter Eustochium, followed Jerome to Bethlehem.
Paula was immensely rich: her property included a whole town. She
gave it all away. She built a monastery in Bethlehem for Jerome; a
nunnery, where she was Abbess and her daughter one of the nuns; and
a guest-house for pilgrims. Here Jerome was Bible instructor to them.
all, and here he completed his work of revising the Latin translation of
the Bible. Jerome wrote about Eustochium, to one of her relatives in
Rome:

> "I wish you could see your niece now. She knows much of the Bible
> by heart. Prayer is her joy. She trains her companions as a choir for
> Christ. (Cf. Ephrem's choir of girls, p. 153). She once was too dainty
> to walk in muddy streets, and had servants to carry her. . . . Now
> (in the guest-house) she trims lamps, sweeps floors, puts cabbage in
> the pot, sets tables, runs to and fro in the service of others. . . . If
> Joseph and Mary came now to Bethlehem, they would find shelter
> and welcome." (70)

And when Paula died, he wrote to Eustochium,

> "Your Mother has left you not one penny, only debts, and crowds
> of needy boys and girls to go on supporting. Eustochium, you have
> received a splendid inheritance." (71)

That was what Jerome wanted to see done with worldly glory.

(c) THE FALLING WORLD

This, through half Jerome's life, was his greatest trouble. When he was
thirty-five, he heard that the Goths had destroyed his home town and
family property. Read again the passages from his later letters (p. 121)
about "a world in ruins", "from Alps to Pyrennees, all laid waste",
"Rome has been sacked". Jerome lived to be seventy-eight. At the end,
in Bethlehem, he was caring for those who were still fleeing from invading barbarians.

11.1 "Many stayed in the shelter of a rock . . . each group had its own trade." (pp. 148, 149)
An early woodcut shows monks making baskets.

11.2 "Jerome struck a blow against worldliness which set all Rome talking. His greatest influence was over a group of ladies." (p. 157)
The picture from a 9th-century Bible shows Jerome explaining the Scriptures to Paula and Eustochium, the "immensely rich" mother and daughter who gave away all their possessions and became nuns.

"North Africa, Egypt, the East, Bethlehem itself, are thronged with penniless refugees. . . . I have had to give up writing my commentary on Ezekiel, and nearly all study. The crowds of homeless made me want to turn the words of Scripture into deeds, not talking about holy things but doing them." (72)

And here one stops being sorry for Jerome and gives thanks to God for him. He left other studies to give himself to the Bible, and now in old age, as a monk, left even Bible studies, to practise that love which the Bible teaches. In doing this, when Roman civilization was falling—and it *was* the end of an age—he was preparing for the future. His Latin Bible, called the "Vulgate" (i.e. the "People's Bible"), was the Bible used among all western Christians for a thousand years. That was Jerome's first contribution: the Bible.

Jerome's second contribution was the Monastery. Though he lived half his life in Bethlehem, Jerome still belonged to, and influenced, the West. His letters praised the monastic life; his own life illustrated the monastery as a centre of civilized living, and a centre to flee to when civilization fell. And the monastery was a place where men had books, where they learned to read and write and copy, while outside in the world most men handled, not a pen, but a sword. Thus the monastery *did* preserve civilization through the West's Dark Ages, and made sure, not only that Europe had a future, but that it had a Christian future. Jerome, who was the most learned man in Christendom, and his great contemporary Augustine (p. 126) have been called "the makers of Latin Christianity". They prepared the way for the Church of the West in the Middle Ages. Here again, (as in the reference, at the end of the previous section, to Persian monks in China) are subjects which will be discussed more fully in another volume of this history.

STUDY SUGGESTIONS

1. "The word 'monk' comes from the Greek *monachos*" (p. 146). What does this Greek word mean?
2. Give the names of two Jewish communities living before the time of Christ whose members were like monks.
3. (a) In what ways was John the Baptist like a monk?
   (b) Suggest two ways in which Jesus was *un*like a monk.
4. (a) What two changes occurred in the fourth and fifth centuries, which encouraged the monastic movement?
   (b) For what two chief reasons did men at that time enter the monastic life?
5. (a) Describe in your own words the sort of man Antony was, and the way in which he lived.

(b) Athanasius called Antony "the model for monks", but Basil regarded the solitary monk as mistaken. What is your opinion?

6. (a) What was the chief difference between the life of the monks who followed Antony, and the life of those who followed Pachomius?

(b) What is meant by each of the following words, as applied to the monastic life?

Community   Rule   Order

7. In which countries did each of the following chiefly live and work?

Antony   Pachomius   Basil   Ephrem

8. (a) Describe briefly the "Rule" which Pachomius laid down for his monks.

(b) Find out all you can about the "Rules" of any modern religious communities (monks or nuns) in your own country. In what ways, if at all, do they differ from the Rule of Pachomius?

(c) What other "communities" of people do you know of today whose lives are organized in accordance with a Rule and an Order?

9. (a) What special sorts of work did Basil's monks undertake?

(b) In what ways was Basil's way of life like that of Jesus?

10. (a) For what special reason was Ephrem in the habit of writing songs and verses?

(b) Some evangelistic groups today use jazz and pop music as a means of drawing crowds to church. Do you think this is a good thing? Do you think it is usually successful? Give your reasons in each case.

11. (a) In what chief way was the character of Jerome different from that of Ephrem or Basil?

(b) It has been said that Jerome had to choose between Cicero and Christ. What does this mean?

(c) Read Amos 3.13–4.5 and the words of Jerome quoted on p. 155. For what kind of behaviour was each reproaching the wealthy congregations and religious leaders of his time?

(d) Give two examples of "worldly" behaviour to which Church leaders may be tempted today.

12. Who were Paula and Eustochium, and how did they use their "worldly glory" to the greater glory of God?

13. What were Jerome's two greatest contributions to the life of the Church?

CHAPTER 12

What Christians today owe to the Early Church

To estimate the debt of Christians today to the Early Church, it might be best to go through all the chapters of this book asking: "What *here* has been added to my Christian inheritance?" The list would be a long one, for we owe much to the Early Church. Such a list, however, is of most value if made by each reader for himself. So we shall make this chapter a short one, dealing with two subjects only: what the Early Church did for us with regard to (a) the Bible, and (b) the Church.

THE BIBLE

"Christianity is Christ." No three-word definition of our religion could say more. And to go on from that, Christ is revealed to us in the New Testament, and the New Testament was secured for us by the Early Church.

Besides the Gospels of Matthew, Mark, Luke, and John, there were other "Gospels". For example, there was one with stories of the childhood of Jesus. It tells of Jesus and His playmates making birds with clay; Jesus claps His hands—and His birds can fly. One boy pushes against Jesus—and the boy drops dead. The four Gospels of the New Testament were established in use long before these other "Gospels" were written. They are not only late in date, but false in the stories they tell. The Jesus of the four Gospels was not a conjurer who might make clay birds seem to fly, nor a wizard who would strike dead someone who touched Him. Their only value is that they make us turn thankfully to the real Gospels, saying, "How different! How true!" The distinguishing of the true Gospels from the false was done for us in this early period, and not the distinguishing of the Gospels only. We were saved also from having false Acts and false Epistles, some of them containing not only foolish stories but false doctrine. The fixing of the New Testament Canon (see p. 57), begun so early, has never been changed, and never been seriously questioned. The Early Church secured for us the New Testament, once and for all.

With regard to the Old Testament, we cannot say that the Church's judgement upon Marcion finally settled all problems. The Christian religion arose within the religion of the Jews, and claims to be its fulfilment. But in many countries of the modern world Christians still have the task of relating their religion to their nation, and to their cultural inheritance, and for some this is a pressing problem.

Some Indian Christians have said, "Jesus came, not to destroy, but to fulfil. To us Indians, Jesus comes as the fulfilment of Hinduism, rather than as fulfilment of the Old Testament prophets."

A theologian of pre-Communist (i.e. Nationalist) China said that Chinese Christians, with their Confucian background, think of Jesus as the greatest ethical teacher, more often than they think of Him as the supreme revelation of God the Father.

African Christians today like to look back, beyond the ancestral spirits, and the many other mysterious powers, to their forefathers' belief in one God over all.

So Christians today may seem to face a question similar to that which was asked by Christians in the second century: "The background for Christ's coming—is it the Old Testament, or something else?" However, modern Christians face this question with a difference. Second-century Christians faced it when it arose for the first time. We have to thank them for both their warning to us and their example. They warn us against those who, like Marcion and the Gnostics, try to change the Christian message to fit their own pattern of thought. They provide the example of men like Clement of Alexandria who recognized that among the Greeks, as well as among the Jews, God had prepared the way for Christ. Thus we may, with Tertullian, thankfully claim the whole Bible as our inheritance:

"This is my property. I have long possessed it. I hold sure title-deeds from the original owners. I am the heir of the Apostles." (73)

We should also give thanks to the Early Church because it began so early to translate the Bible. By the year 200, the number of languages containing the Scriptures had advanced from one, Greek, to four, adding Syriac for the east, Coptic for the south, and Latin for the west. Four more languages were added soon after 400: Armenian, Georgian, Ethiopic, Gothic; and most surprising of all, soon after 500, a language of the Huns (pp. 125, 126).

Few people today realize that it was missionaries of the Early Church, making scripts in order to translate the Scriptures, who were responsible for the beginning of literature among the Teutonic (Germanic) peoples of northern Europe, including the English, and even influenced some languages of East Asia.

Similarly few people recognize the Church's contribution to literacy, which came about because the religion of a Book demanded that, where possible, its followers should learn to read. These achievements of the Early Church may seem small compared with what the Church has done more recently. Between 1800 and the present day the Scriptures have been translated into more than 1,000 languages, and very many of these languages have been given writing for the first time. But we should indeed be thankful for the example set *so early*. Some people may brush aside as false exaggeration the words of Eusebius quoted on p. 81, but it is wiser to acknowledge them as true foresight about a task already well begun:

> "God gave power to the Apostles, so that what they wrote should be translated into every language, civilized and barbarous; should be read and pondered by all nations; and . . . received as the revelation of God." (Young **218**)

THE CHURCH

We shall consider two aspects of the Church: continuity and expansion. First, *continuity: the succession of Christian lives.*

As well as the Bible, containing the Old Testament and the New, we have the Church coming down to us from Christ through His Apostles. This is what Clement of Alexandria says about it.

> "God, who revealed himself through the incarnation of Jesus Christ, has always loved to clothe himself with man, in ancient times clothing himself with the Prophets, now *clothing himself with the Church*." (74)

If we think this doctrine gives too much importance to the Church, we should consider the words of an Indian enquirer, who knew nothing of the Church at all. He had read the New Testament, with no one to help him. The picture of Jesus in the Gospels fascinated him. The sufferings and death of Jesus deeply moved him.

> "Then he read on, and saw the scene change. The Gospels told about Jesus, his works, his sufferings. The Acts told what the disciples did and thought and taught. The Church continued where Jesus had left off. 'Therefore,' said this man to me, 'I must belong to *the Church* which *carries on the life of Christ*'." (75)

Perhaps if we consider the Church today, we can see this continuity most clearly. Some people are Christians because they grew up in a Christian family; others are Christians because they were influenced by a Christian friend. In both cases a Christian life springs from a Christian life. There is *a succession of Christian lives* which, *starting from Jesus and His Apostles*, has come through more than sixty generations, and has reached to you and me. This is one aspect of the Church: this is our spiritual ancestry.

The period of the Early Church was one of special danger. The succession of Christian lives might have been broken. Christian lives not only continued, however, but in this period shone brightly, and

12.1 "What the apostles wrote should be translated into every language." (p. 162)
"Missionaries of the early Church were responsible for the beginning of literature."
(p. 161)
The Bible Societies carry on this responsibility today: these two translators are
working together in Fiji.

12.2 "The fact of Christianity as a world religion." (p. 166)
Delegates from 235 Church bodies and all six continents attended the fourth
Assembly of the World Council of Churches at Uppsala, Sweden, in 1968.

were well recorded. The records of this period have strengthened Christians of later generations—including our own—when called upon to endure opposition and persecution. In thinking of the Church's "noble army of martyrs" it is natural to turn to the New Testament, but the New Testament contains little about them. The first martyr is mentioned there, Stephen, who, like his Master, said of his persecutors: "Lord do not hold this sin against them" (Acts 7.60). There is the brief note about James, son of Zebedee: "Herod killed him with the sword" (Acts 12.2). The Revelation begins with one name, "Antipas, my witness, my faithful one, who was killed among you", i.e. at Pergamum, but with no details (Rev. 2.13). Later comes the vision of a white-robed multitude in heaven "who have come out of great tribulation" (Rev. 7.14); and a dreadful picture of the persecuting Roman State on earth, "drunk with the blood of the saints, and the blood of the martyrs of Jesus". But no details are given about any of them at all.

We have far more information about the lives of saints and heroes from the second century onward. These are our ancestors in the family of the Church.

With regard to the Church's *expansion*, let us turn again to Origen. The anti-Christian Celsus had asked:

"What new thing has happened, since the crucifixion, which might make us believe that Jesus was the Son of God?" (76)

In replying, Origen turned to Isaiah 66.8:

"Who has heard such a thing?
Who has seen such things?
Shall a land be born in one day?
Shall a nation be brought forth in one moment?"

Origen wrote:

"A new thing has happened—the multitudinous rise of the 'nation' of the Christians, as if 'brought forth in one moment'." (77)

(Compare Bardaisan, Tertullian, and Origen on p. 35.)

Here was "a new thing" for believers, as well as for men like Celsus. The Gospel from the beginning was that "God so loved *the world*" (John 3.16). The Lord's commission to His followers was "Go into all *the world*" (Mark 16.15). The Acts of the Apostles begins the history of the Church's *world* mission, but of only one part of it, and in one direction.

THE WORLD MISSION

We have been able, in these chapters, to follow the continued mission, as it spread north, south, east, and west. We have come to know, and, in some cases, to receive memorable words from, missionaries at work in ever-widening areas of three continents, Europe, Africa, and Asia. America and Australia had not yet been discovered by the people of what is now called the "old" world. Thus Europe, Africa, and Asia were then the extent of the known world. The Early Church established Christianity as a "world" religion, and, as Origen said, this was "a new fact".

What difference does the Early Church's wide outreaching make to Christians of the twentieth century?

Take India, for example. Mr Nehru was not a Christian, but he was able to assure the Portuguese in Goa that Christians needed no foreign protector. "I recall", he said, "that there were Christians in India before there were Christians in Portugal." The Church of South India (founded in 1947) has wisely included in its Liturgy some items preserved from ancient times by the Syrian Orthodox Church. It is good for Christians of all traditions to know and claim kinship with the Early Church as it survives and flourishes in Kerala (pp. 112, 113).

In the previous chapter we saw the Persian monks moving towards China, but not yet arrived (p. 154). The song of the angels in Luke 2.14 was expanded into a hymn which was called the Morning Hymn by the Greeks, "Glory to God in the highest", and which was translated for the west into Latin, *Gloria in excelsis Deo*. This hymn early travelled eastwards in a Syriac form. In the dry climate of north-west China a sheet of paper has survived for twelve hundred years, with the same Syriac hymn put into beautiful Chinese verse. It is hymn number one in the hymnbook used by many modern Churches in China. Christianity has been misunderstood, not only by non-Christian Chinese, but by Christians also, as being a part of "western" culture. But here is something from the Early Church which was written in Chinese seven centuries before America was discovered, and seven centuries before the hymn was translated from Latin into English for the English Prayerbook.

The African continent is full of associations with the Early Church—Tertullian, Cyprian, Clement, Origen, Augustine and the rest—which all African Christians should know and claim. The ancient Churches of Egypt and Ethiopia contributed much, especially Ethiopia, which has been a Christian-ruled country since 350 (p. 107), the oldest in the world. This ancient African Church should contribute a sense of the past, of an African past, to African Churches of recent foundation. When ancient Churches and modern Churches get to know, and begin to learn from, each other, it is to the benefit of both.

We may hope that Christians of Arab race will come to remember and repeat the prayer of the 177 Christian women of Najran, fourteen centuries ago: "Grant us the power to walk our way of martyrdom"

(p. 110); and that Christians in Persia, when on Good Friday they remember the Passion of our Lord, may remember too their Bishop Shimun and his hundred fellow-martyrs. And there in the background are another sixteen thousand Persian Christians whose names were once recorded in Ctesiphon, and who are for ever "written in the Lamb's Book of Life" (Rev. 21.27) (p. 99).

Even if we added many further illustrations, some Christians would still feel left out because they have no relics from a Christian past, no record of the Early Church in, or even approaching, their own land. But the fact of Christianity as a world religion does not depend on geography; it is an inheritance which all Christians share. Wherever we are, we continue our work and our witness, believing that there is no country where the Church is foreign, because God's will is that it should come to every land. We are not transplanting a religion to countries where it does not belong. We are working to make up for previous delays and failures in the outreaching of the universal Church which is the fulfilling of the eternal will of God.

STUDY SUGGESTIONS

1. Make a list of what you yourself think that Christians today owe to the Early Church.
   (This could be done in three ways:
   (a) From memory of what you have read in this book;
   (b) By looking again quickly at each chapter and asking yourself "What *here* has been added to my Christian inheritance?"; or
   (c) By thinking of your own life as a Christian and the life of the Church to which you belong, and asking yourself "What is there here, which has been handed down from the time of Paul—or of Justin or Jerome?")
2. "To Indians, Jesus comes as the fulfilment of Hinduism rather than . . . of the Old Testament prophets" (p. 125).
   To what extent is the same thing true of the national or traditional culture and religion of your own country?
3. (a) What kind of warning, and (b) what kind of example do the Christians of the second century provide for modern Christians who face the question: "The background for Christ's coming, is it the Old Testament, or something else?"
4. (a) Find out the number of languages in your country into which all or part of the Bible has been translated, when the translations were first made, and by whom.
   (b) "Missionaries of the early Church were responsible for the beginning of literature among the peoples of Northern Europe. Similarly . . . the Church's contribution to literacy happened because

the religion of a Book demanded that its followers should learn to read." (p. 161)

Find out:

(i) When the earliest written literature in your own language came into being;

(ii) What part, if any, Christian missionaries played in the development of literacy among the people of your country.

5. In what way has a knowledge of the history of the early Church strengthened Christians of later generations to endure opposition and persecution?

6. (a) What did Origen reply when the anti-Christian Celsus asked: "What new thing has happened which might make us believe that Jesus was the Son of God?"

(b) Give an example of anything which has happened in modern times, either in your own country or elsewhere, to make non-Christians believe that Jesus is the Son of God.

7. (a) Find out when the first Christians came to your country.

(b) Find out at what dates the different Churches in your country became formally constituted.

(c) What influence if any do you think the Churches have had on the political or economic development of your country?

8. Look through any hymn book, either in your own language or any other language of your country, which gives sources of the hymns. See how many are translations from the writings of early Christians, and how many were composed by members of a local Church.

9. "There is no country where the Church is foreign" (p. 166)

(a) What is meant by this statement?

(b) How far do you think that Christians in your country would agree that it is true?

References for Quotations
from Source Materials which are
not included in Young's "Handbook"

Throughout this book quotation reference numbers in *bold* type correspond to the reference numbers of extracts from source materials included in W. G. Young's *Handbook of Source Materials for Students of Church History* (see Bibliography, p. 171).

Quotation reference numbers in brackets correspond to the references listed below.

REFERENCE NUMBER	AUTHOR (IF KNOWN)	SOURCE
(1)		*History of the Later Han Dynasty*
(2)	Strabo	*Geography*
(3)	Tertullian	*On Baptism* 2
(4)	Tertullian	*On Baptism* 1
(5)		*The Passion of Perpetua and Felicitas*
(6)	Tertullian	*To the Nations* 8
(7)	Origen	*Commentary on Ezekiel*
(8)	Eusebius	*Ecclesiastical History* III 1
(9)		*Teaching of the Twelve Apostles* 11
(10)	Lucian of Samosata	*On the Death of Peregrinus* 13
(11)		*Teaching of the Twelve Apostles* 4
(12)	Tertullian	*To Scapula* 5
(13)	Eusebius	*Ecclesiastical History* XIV 7
(14)	Celsus	*Origen Against Celsus* VII 18
(15)	Tertullian	*Confutation of Heretics* 36
(16)	Irenaeus	*Against Heresies* I 10
(17)		*The World Mission of the Church* (Report of Tambaram Madras Missionary Conference 1938), p. 53
(18)	Clement of Alexandria	*Miscellanies* VII 10 (abbreviated)
(19)	Clement of Alexandria	*Miscellanies* VII 1
(20)	Eusebius	*Ecclesiastical History* V 17

(21)	Ignatius	*Letter to the Ephesians* 4
(22)	Minucius Felix	*Octavius* 6
(23)	Ignatius	*Letter to the Romans* 5
(24)	Tertullian	*Apology* 2
(25)	Eusebius	*Ecclesiastical History* V 1
(26)	Origen	*Against Celsus* VII 68
(27)	Origen	*Against Celsus* III 15
(28)		*The Martyrdom of Pionius* (Kidd *Documents Illustrative of the History of the Church* Vol. I p. 187)
(29)	Cyprian	*On the Lapsed* 8
(30)	Cyprian	*On the Lapsed* 13
(31)	Cyprian	*On the Lapsed* 2
(32)	Eusebius	*Life of Constantine* I 28
(33)	Eusebius	*Oration in Praise of Constantine* 17
(34)	Eusebius	*Life of Constantine* IV 36
(35)	Eusebius	*Ecclesiastical History* I 13
(36)	Eusebius	*Ecclesiastical History* I 13
(37)	Eusebius	*Ecclesiastical History* IX 8
(38)	Eusebius	*Life of Constantine* IV 56
(39)	Sozomen	*Church History* I 1
(40)	John Foster	*Travel Diary*
(41)	Jerome	*Letter* 60
(42)	Jerome	*Letter* 127
(43)	Sozomen	*Church History* VI 37
(44)	Philostorgius	*Church History* II 5
(45)	Chrysostom	*Homilies*
(46)	Jerome	*Letter* 107
(47)	Augustine	*The City of God* XII 22
(48)	Origen	*Against Celsus* III 52
(49)	Lactantius	*Divine Institutes* V 20
(50)	Justin	I *Apology* 5
(51)	Tatian	*To the Greeks* 5
(52)	Eusebius	*Life of Constantine* 7
(53)	Socrates	*Church History* I 8
(54)	Socrates	*Church History* VII 48
(55)	Tertullian	*On Flight in Persecution* 1
(56)	Sozomen	*Church History* I 13

REFERENCES FOR QUOTATIONS

(57)	Athanasius	*Life of Antony*
(58)	Sozomen	*Church History* III 14
(59)	Basil	W. K. Lowther Clarke *Ascetic Works of St Basil*, p. 163
(60)	Gregory of Nazianzus	*Orations* 43
(61)	Sozomen	*Church History* VI 33
(62)	Sozomen	*Church History* VI 33
(63)	Ephrem	*Greek Works* I 129
(64)	Sozomen	*Church History* III 16
(65)	Sozomen	*Church History* VI 34
(66)	Ephrem	*Greek Works* II 396
(67)	Jerome	*Letter* 22 (30)
(68)	Jerome	Ammianus Marcellinus *Res Gestae* (Things Done) XXVII 3
(69)	Jerome	*Letter* 22 (16)
(70)	Jerome	*Letters* 54, 66
(71)	Jerome	*Letter* 108
(72)	Jerome	*Commentary on Ezekiel* Preface
(73)	Tertullian	*Confutation of Heretics*, 37
(74)	Clement of Alexandria	*Selections from the Prophetic Sayings* 23
(75)	Azariah	*Tambaram Madras Series* Vol. VII
(76)	Celsus	Origen *Against Celsus* VIII 41
(77)	Origen	*Against Celsus* VIII 43

Bibliography

Readers may find the following books useful for further study:

INTRODUCTORY BOOKS

After the Apostles John Foster. ANZEA Scripture Union, Sydney

An Introduction to the History of the Christian Church W. W. Biggs. Arnold, London

The Early Church (Pelican History of the Church Vol 1) Henry Chadwick. Penguin, London

From Jerusalem to New Delhi (Parts 1–3) M. E. Gibbs. Christian Literature Society, Madras

Christianity through the Ages K. S. Latourette. Harper and Row, New York and London

History of the Early Church J. W. C. Wand. Methuen, London

The Christian Fathers Maurice Wiles. Hodder and Stoughton, London

Faithful Witnesses E. R. Hardy. Lutterworth, London

Persecution in the Early Church H. B. Workman. Epworth, London

MORE ADVANCED BOOKS

The History of Christianity R. H. Bainton. Nelson, London, New York

A History of the Early Church H. Lietzmann. Lutterworth, London and World Publishing Co, New York

SOURCE AND REFERENCE BOOKS

A Handbook of Source Materials for Students of Church History (Indian Theological Library) W. G. Young. Christian Literature Society, Madras and Lutterworth, London

Documents of the Christian Church H. S. Bettenson, Oxford University Press, New York

A New Eusebius and *Creeds, Councils, and Controversies* H. Stevenson. S.P.C.K., London

(*Documents Illustrative of the History of the Church* B. J. Kidd. S.P.C.K., London Out of print but available in many libraries)

Dictionary of Christian Biography Ed. W. Smith and H. Wace. Little, Brown, Boston

Oxford Dictionary of the Christian Church F. L. Cross. Oxford University Press, London and New York

Atlas of the Early Christian World F. van der Meer and Christine Mohrmann. Nelson, London and New York

FILMSTRIP

The Spread of Christianity: 1 The Winning of the Roman Empire John Foster, Common Ground Longman, London

Key to Study Suggestions

CHAPTER 1

1. See p. 2 lines 19–29.
2. See maps on pp. xii and 43.
3. (a) see page 1 para. 3 (last line).
   (b) See p. 3 para. 5, and following pages.
4. See p. 5.
5. (a) See p. 6 last para. and p. 7 paras. 1 and 2.
6. (a) See p. 7 para. 4.
   (b) See p. 7 last para. and p. 12 first para.
   (c) See p. 12 para. 4.
7. (a) See p. 3 last para. and p. 5 first para.
   (b) See p. 13 para. 1.
8. See p. 13 para. 3.
9. See p. 15 para. 2.
10. Based on pp. 13 and 15.
11. See pp. 15–17.
12. (a) See p. 6 para. 3.
    (b) See p. 3 last para.
    (c) See p. 16 para. 3 last 5 lines.

CHAPTER 2

1. (a) See p. 19 para. 1.
   (b) See p. 19 para. 3 and p. 20 paras. 1 and 2.
2. (a) See p. 20 para. 5.
   (b) See p. 20 para. 4.
3. (a) See p. 20 para. 3.
   (b) Acts 16.40 and Col. 4.15.
   (c) See Acts 18.1 and 2; Acts 18.24–26; Rom. 16.3–5
       Corinth, Rome, Ephesus.
4. (a) See p. 20 last line and p. 21 first para.
   (c) See p. 21 first para.
   (d) See p. 21 first para.
5. (a) See p. 25 last line and p. 27 lines 1 and 2.
   (b) See p. 31 last para.
   (c) See p. 23 last para. and p. 24 paras. 1 and 2.
   (d) See p. 32 para. 3.
6. Based on pp. 25 and 27, section headed "Eucharist".
   Some possible answers might be:
   (a) The Words of Institution, i.e. those used to consecrate the Bread and Wine,
   were the words used by Jesus Himself at the Last Supper.
   A collection was made of money or gifts for the poor.
   (b) Most of the prayers were not yet in a set form.
7. See p. 25 para. 2.
8. Based on p. 30, section headed "Teaching on how to pray".
9. (a) (i) See p. 31 para. 3. (ii) See p. 32 para. 5.
   (b) See p. 31 para. 4.
10. Based on p. 23 last para. and p. 24 paras. 1 and 2.

11. (a) Both refer to a splendid "being" (perhaps Christ in glory) with white hair, and to multitudes of people (perhaps those who died in faith) clothed in white.
(b) See p. 28 end of last para.

CHAPTER 3

1. Bardaisan:
(a) and (b) See p. 35 para. 2.   (c) See p. 86 last para.
Tertullian:
(a), (b) and (c) See p. 23 line 19 to p. 24 para. 1.
Eusebius:
(a), (b) and (c) See p. 40 para. 4.
Gregory the "Wonder-Worker":
(a), (b) and (c) See p. 45 para. 2.
2. See p. 49 section headed "Confessors and Martyrs".
3. (a) See p. 40 last para.
(b) See p. 41 first para.
(c) See p. 41 first para.
4. See p. 35 lines 28–33.
5. (a) and (b) See p. 35 para. 3.
6. (a) and (b) See p. 36 para. 3.
7. See p. 36 para. 2.
8. (a) See p. 36 para. 3.
(b) See p. 36 para. 4.
9. (a) See p. 38 para. 4.
(b) See p. 38 para. 4.
11. (a) and (b) See p. 40 first para.
12. (a) and (b) See p. 41 paras. 1 and 2.
(c) and (d) See p. 41 para. 3.
13. (a) See p. 42 para. 3.
15. See p. 45 para. 2.
21. See p. 50 para. 3.

CHAPTER 4

1. (a) Marcionites, Gnostics, Montanists.
(b) See p. 53 para. 1.
2. (a) *Fel:* gall (bitterness)   *Mel:* honey (sweetness)
Gnosis: knowledge   *Episcopos:* bishop
Presbuteros: presbyter
(b) See p. 57 para. 2.
3. See p. 56 para. 2.
4. (a) See p. 54 last para. and p. 56 lines 1 and 2.
(b) See p. 56 para. 3.
6. (a) (i) See p. 57 para. 4.   (ii) See p. 57 para. 5.   (iii) See p. 57 para. 6.
(b) See p. 58 para. 2.
7. See p. 58 para. 2.
8. See p. 58 para. 4 and p. 59.
9. (a) See p. 60 para. 2, lines 4–7.
(b) See p. 5, line 1.
(c) Based on p. 60 last para. and p. 61 first para.
10. (a) See p. 61 last para.
(b) See p. 62 first para.
11. (a) See p. 61 paras. 4 and 5.
(b) See p. 62 para. 2.
12. (a) See p. 62 para. 3, last 2 lines.
(b) See p. 62 para. 4.
13. (a) and (b) See p. 63 para. 2.
(c) See p. 63

CHAPTER 5

1. (a) and (b) See p. 66 paras. 2 and 3.
2. (a) See p. 66 last para. and p. 67 para. 2.
   (b) See p. 67 para. 3.
3. (a) The master was to protect the slave and not oppress him in any way.
   (b) Slaves should serve their masters as they would Christ, and masters should treat their slaves fairly, knowing they also have a master in heaven.
4. (a) See p. 67 para. 5 line 3.
   (b) See p. 71 last line and p. 72 lines 1 and 2.
   (c) See p. 71 para. 3 line 6.
   (d) Cyprian: see p. 67 para. 2.
       Ignatius: see p. 72 line 8.
       Domitilla: see p. 73 last line.
   (e) See p. 74 last 3 lines.
   (f) See p. 74 para. 2 lines 1–3.
5. (a) See p. 68 para. 3.
6. See p. 67 paras. 4 and 5.
7. See p. 71 para 3.
8. See p. 76 para. 6 lines 4–6.
9. (a), (b) and (c) See p. 76 last para. and p. 78 first para.
10. (a) See p. 78 para. 4.
    (b) See pp. 79 and 81.
11. (a) and (b) See p. 72 para. 3.
    (c) See p. 73 para. 1.
12. (a) and (b) See p. 81 last 5 lines.
13. (a) and (b) See p. 81 para. 1.

CHAPTER 6

2. (a) See p. 85 para. 2.
   (b) See p. 85 para. 3.
3. (a) and (b) See p. 85 para. 4.
4. (a) See p. 85 last para.
   (b) See p. 86 para. 3.
   (c) See p. 86 para. 4.
   (d) See p. 86 para. 1.
5. (a) See p. 86 para. 4 line 4.
   (b) See p. 86 para. 4 line 4 ff.
6. (a) Based on p. 87 para. 2.
7. (a) See p. 89 para. 2.
   (b) See p. 89 para. 2 lines 18–21.
   (c) Based on p. 89 last para. and p. 90 para. 1.
8. (a), (b) and (c) See p. 90 para. 2 lines 1–6.
9. (a) See p. 90 para. 2 lines 15–17.
   (b) See p. 90 para. 2 last line.
10. (a) See p. 90 para. 2.

CHAPTER 7

2. (a) See p. 92 para. 3 line 2.
   (b) See p. 92 lines 12 and 13.
   (c) See p. 92 lines 13 and 14.
3. (a) See p. 92 para. 3 lines 1 and 2.
   (b) See p. 92 para. 3 lines 2 and 3.
   (c) See p. 92 para. 3 line 4.
4. (a) See p. 93 section headed "One of the first converts: Paqida in the year 99".
   (b) See p. 93 section headed "The first martyr, Samsun, in the year 123".
5. (a) See p. 93 para. 3 lines 8 and 9.

6. (a) See p. 94 para. 1.
   (b) (i) and (ii) See p. 94 para. 2.
7. See p. 94 para. 3 lines 1–6.
8. See p. 94 para. 3 lines 7–11.
9. (a) and (b) See p. 95 para. 2.
10. (a) and (b) See p. 95 para. 3.
11. (a), (b) and (c) See p. 95 last para.
12. (a) See p. 97 para. 3 lines 4–12.
    (b) See p. 97 para. 3 line 13 and p. 98 para. 1.
14. (a) See p. 99 last para. and p. 100 line 6.
    (b) See p. 100 lines 6–12.
15. (a) See p. 100 lines 13–18.
    (b) See p. 100 para. 2.
16. (a) See p. 102 last para. lines 4–10.
    (b) See p. 103 first para.

CHAPTER 8

1. (a) See p. 106 para. 2.
   (b) See p. 106 line 30 and p. 107 para. 3.
   (c) See p. 107 para. 4.
2. (a) and (b) See p. 107 para. 2.
3. (a) See p. 107 para. 5.
   (b) See p. 107 para. 6.
   (c) See p. 107 last 2 paras.
4. See p. 109 paras. 2 and 3.
6. See p. 109 para. 3 lines 7–9.
7. St Thomas: See p. 112 section headed "St Thomas the Apostle".
   Pantaenus: See p. 113 section headed "Pantaenus about 180".
   David: See p. 113 section headed "David, Bishop of Basra, about 300".
   John: See p. 113 section headed "John the 'Persian' 325".
   Thomas: See p. 113 section headed "Thomas the Merchant, 345".
   Pallivanavar: See p. 114 section headed "Pallivanavar, about 350".
   Cosmas: See p. 114 section headed "Cosmas the 'India Sailor' ".
8. See p. 112 para. 4.

CHAPTER 9

2. See p. 117 para. 1.
3. (a) See p. 117 para. 2 lines 1–7.
   (b) See p. 117 para. 2 lines 7–9.
4. (a) See p. 117 para. 2 line 9 and para. 4.
   (b) See p. 119 paras. 3 and 4.
   (c) See p. 117 para. 3 and p. 119 para. 1.
   (d) See p. 117 para. 2 and p. 119 para. 3.
   (e) See p. 119 para. 4 lines 1–4.
5. AD 312: See p. 126 para. 5 line 10.
   AD 410: See p. 119 para. 4 lines 11 and 12.
   AD 480: See p. 117 last para.
6. Ulfilas: See p. 122 para. 2.
   Chrysostom: See p. 124 para. 3 lines 3 and 4.
   Qaradushat: See p. 125 lines 30 and 31.
7. (a) See p. 124 last para.
   (b) See p. 122 lines 12 and 13.
   (c) See p. 122 lines 14–29.
8. (a) See p. 125 para. 1.
9. (a) Based on p. 124 lines 24–29.
   (b) Based on p. 124 para. 2 last 4 lines.
10. (a) and (b) See p. 126 para. 2.
11. (b) See p. 124 sections 1, 2 and 3, p. 129 section 4.

CHAPTER 10

1. (a) Teaching   tenet
2. (a) See p. 131 last line and p. 132 para. 1.
   (b) See p. 132 para. 2.
3. See p. 133 para. 1.
4. See p. 134 para. 3, lines 20–23.
5. Justin: see p. 13 para. 5, line 1.
   Tatian: see p. 85 last para. and p. 86 para. 4.
   Origen: see p. 3 last para.
   Lactantius: see p. 133 para. 2.
   Arius: see p. 138 paras. 3 and 4.
   Nestorius: see p. 141 para. 2.
6. (a) Based on p. 135 para. 3.
   (b) See p. 135 para. 5.
7. (a) Based on p. 133 lines 33–40.
8. (a) See p. 137 para. 4 last 2 lines.
9. (a) See p. 137 paras. 5 and 6 and p. 138 para. 4.
   (b) See p. 138 para. 4 lines 5 and 6.
   (c) See p. 138 para. 5 and p. 139 para. 1.
10. (a) See p. 139 para. 2.
   (b) See p. 138 para. 3 and p. 139 para. 2.
   (c) See p. 140 para. 2.
11. (a) Antioch: see p. 140 section (1).
   Alexandria: see p. 140 section (2).
   Rome: see p. 141 section (3).
   (b) See p. 141 para. 2.
12. (a) and (b) see p. 143 para. 2.
   (d) See p. 141 section (3).

CHAPTER 11

1. See p. 146 para. 1.
2. See p. 146 para. 3.
3. (a) See p. 146 para. 3 last 3 lines.
   (b) See p. 146 para. 4.
4. (a) and (b) See p. 147 para. 2.
5. (a) See p. 147 para. 4 and p. 148 para. 4.
6. (a) See p. 148 para. 5.
   (b) See p. 148 last para. and p. 149.
7. See sub-headings on pp. 147, 148, 151, 152.
8. (a) See p. 149 section headed "Rule".
9. (a) and (b) See p. 151 last para. and p. 152 para. 1.
10. (a) See p. 153 lines 6–13.
11. (a) See p. 154 para. 3.
   (b) See p. 154 section numbered (a).
   (c) See p. 155 para. 4 line 1.
12. See p. 156 para. 3.
13. See p. 158 lines 7–21.

CHAPTER 12

3. (a) and (b) See p. 161 para. 5.
5. See p. 162 last para. and p. 164 para. 1.
6. (a) See p. 164 para. 3.
9. See p. 166 last para.

Index

177